Ilya Grigoryev

# AnyLogic 6
# in Three Days

## A quick course in simulation modeling

**First edition**

AnyLogic North America
2012

Cataloging-in-Publication data for this book is available from the Library of Congress.

ISBN-13: 978-0615705675

ISBN-10: 0615705677

## Preface

This is the first practical textbook on AnyLogic 6 from AnyLogic developers. AnyLogic is the unique simulation software tool that supports three simulation modeling methods: system dynamics, discrete event, and agent based modeling and allows you to create multi-method models.

This book is based on our 3-day AnyLogic Fundamentals training. The book is structured around four examples: a manufacturing model, a warehouse model, a model of a consumer market, and an epidemic model. We also give some theory on different modeling methods.

You can consider this book as your first guide in studying AnyLogic. Having read this book and completed the exercises, you will be able to create discrete event models using process flowcharts, to draw stock and flow diagrams, and to build simple agent based models.

## Acknowledgements

I would like first to thank Timofey Popkov for the idea to adopt the training materials to a book and for his help in writing the book. I also thank Andrei Borshchev for numerous contributions to the book and Sergey Suslov for helpful suggestions.

Please let me know how I can improve the book.

*Ilya V. Grigoryev*
grigoryev@anylogic.com

# Contents

# Modeling and simulation modeling

This chapter is from "The Book of AnyLogic" (working title) being currently written by Dr. Andrei Borshchev and partially available on AnyLogic website.

Modeling is one of the ways to solve real-world problems. In many cases, we can't afford to find the right solutions by experimenting with real objects: building, destroying, making changes may be too expensive, dangerous, or just impossible. If this is so, we leave the real world and go to the world of models as shown in the figure below. We build a model of a real system: its representation in a modeling language. This process assumes abstraction: we omit the details we think are irrelevant and we keep those we think are important. The model is always less complex than the original system.

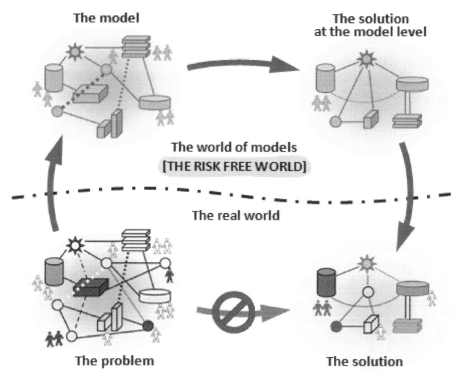

Modeling

♦ **The model-building phases - mapping the real world to the world of models, choosing the abstraction level, and choosing the modeling language are less formalized than the process of using models to solve problems. This is still more an art than a science.**

After we have built the model – and sometimes even as we build the model – we start to explore and understand the original system's structure and behavior, test how the system will behave under a variety of conditions, play and compare scenarios, and optimize. After we find our solution, we then can map it to the real world.

♦ **The whole modeling thing is actually about finding the way from the problem to its solution through a risk-free world where we are allowed to make mistakes, undo things, go back in time, and start over again.**

## Types of models

There are many types of models, including the mental models we each use to understand how things work in the real world: friends, family, colleagues, car drivers, town where you live, things that you buy, economy, sports, politics, or your own body. Decisions such as what to say to your child, what to eat for breakfast, who to vote for, or where to take your girlfriend are all based on mental models.

Computers are extensively used for modeling, and they provide us with a flexible virtual world where we can easily create anything imaginable. Of course, there are many different types of computer models, from spreadsheets that allow anyone to model expenses to simulation modeling tools that help users explore dynamic systems such as consumer markets and battlefields.

## Analytical vs. simulation modeling

If you could ask a major organization's strategic planning, sales forecasting, logistics, marketing, or project management teams about their preferred modeling tools and technologies, you'd quickly find Microsoft Excel is the most popular modeling software. Excel has obvious advantages: you can find it on any office computer and it is very easy to use. It's also extensible: you can add scripts to your formulas as the spreadsheet logic becomes more sophisticated.

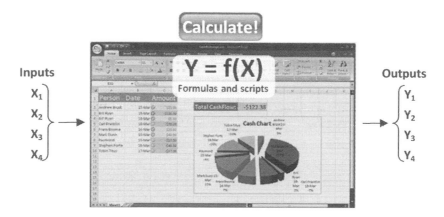

**Analytical model (Excel spreadsheet)**

The technology behind spreadsheet-based modeling is simple: you enter the model inputs in some cells and you view the outputs in others. The input and output values linked by chains of formulas and – in more complex models – scripts. Various add-ons allow you to perform parameter variation, Monte Carlo, or optimization experiments.

However, there's also a large class of problems where the analytic (formula-based) solution doesn't exist or it is very hard to find. This class includes *dynamic systems* that feature:

- Non-linear behavior

- "Memory"

- Non-intuitive influences between variables

- Time and causal dependencies

- All above combined with uncertainty and large number of parameters

In most cases, it's impossible to obtain the right formulas, much less put together a mental model of such a system.

As an example, consider a problem that requires you to optimize a rail or truck fleet. Factors such as travel schedules, loading and unloading times, delivery time restrictions, and terminal point capacities make it difficult to approach with a spreadsheet. A vehicle's availability at a particular location on a particular date at a particular time depends on a sequence of preceding events - and answering the question of where to send the vehicle when it is idle requires us to analyze future event sequences.

◆ **Formulas that are good for expressing static dependencies between variables typically don't do well in describing systems with dynamic behavior. It's why we use another modeling technology - simulation modeling - to analyze dynamic systems.**

*Simulation model* is always an *executable model*: you can *run* it and it will build you a trajectory of the system's state changes. Think of a simulation model as a set of rules that tell you how to move from the system's current state to the following state. The rules can take many forms, including differential equations, statecharts, process flowcharts, and schedules. The model's outputs are produced and observed as the model runs.

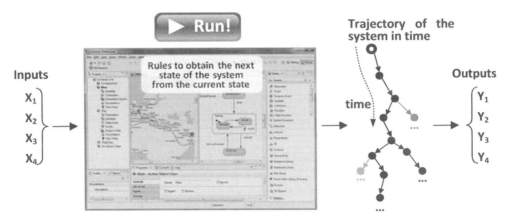

### Simulation model

Simulation modeling is done with special software tools that use simulation-specific languages, both graphic and textual. While it typically requires some training, your time and effort pays off when you create a high quality analysis of a dynamic system.

People - especially those who count themselves as Excel professionals and have some programming background - often still try to build spreadsheet models of dynamic systems. As they try to capture more and more detail, they inevitably start reproducing the functionality of simulators in Excel. The resulting models are slow and unmanageable, and they are usually quickly thrown away.

Virtually any of those details are impossible to capture in an analytic solution. Even if there were formulas to guide your configuration, a small process change could void them, and you'd need a professional mathematician to fix them.

### Advantages of simulation modeling

There are six advantages to simulation modeling:

1. Simulation models enable you to analyze systems and find solutions where methods such as analytic calculations and linear programming fail.

2. After you've chosen an abstraction level, developing a simulation model is simpler than developing an analytical model. It typically requires less intellectual effort, and it is scalable, incremental, and modular.

3. A simulation model's structure naturally reflects the system's structure. Since simulation models are developed using mostly visual languages, it's easy to communicate the model's internals to others.

4. In a simulation model, you can measure values and track entities that are not below the level of abstraction, and you can add measurements and statistical analysis at any time.

5. The ability to play and animate the system behavior in time is one of simulation's great advantages. Animation is used not only for demonstrations, but also for verification and debugging.

6. Simulation models are far more convincing than Excel spreadsheets. If you use a simulation to support your proposal, you'll have an advantage over those who only use numbers.

## *Applications of simulation modeling. Level of abstraction.*

Simulation modeling has accumulated a large number of success stories in very wide and diverse range of application areas. As new modeling methods and technologies emerge and computer power grows, you can expect simulation to enter an ever-larger number of areas.

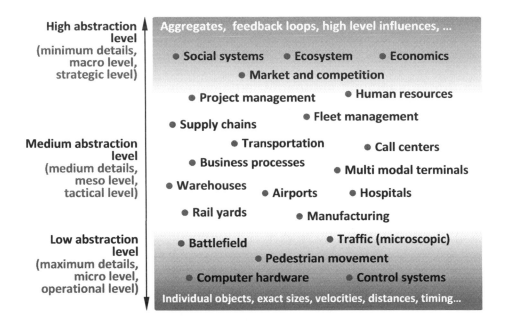

**Applications of simulation**

In the Figure above, you see some simulation applications sorted by the abstraction level of the corresponding models. At the bottom are physical-level models where real world objects are represented with maximum details. At this level, we care about physical interaction, dimensions, velocities, distances, and timings. An automobile's anti-lock brakes, the evacuation of football fans from a stadium, the traffic at an intersection controlled by a traffic light, and soldiers' interaction on the battlefield are examples of problems that require low abstraction modeling.

The models at the top are highly abstract, and they typically use aggregates such as consumer populations and employment statistics rather than individual objects. Since their objects interact at a high level, they can help us understand relationships - such as how the money our company spends on advertising influences our sales - without modeling the intermediate steps.

Other models have an intermediate abstraction level. If we a model a hospital's emergency department, we may care about physical space if we want to know how long it takes to walk from the emergency room to an x-ray station, but physical interaction among people in the building is irrelevant because we assume the building is uncongested.

In a model of a business process or a call center, we model operations' sequence and duration rather than where they take place. In a transportation model, we carefully consider truck or rail car speed, but in a higher level supply chain model, we simply assume an order takes from seven to ten days to arrive.

◆ Choosing the right abstraction level is critical to your modeling project's success. After you decide what to include and what is left below the level of abstraction, it's not difficult to choose your modeling method.

◆ In the model development process, it's normal and even desirable to periodically reconsider the abstraction level. In most cases, you start at a high abstraction level and then add details as you need them.

## The three methods in simulation modeling

In modern simulation modeling, we use three methods: discrete event, agent based, and system dynamics.

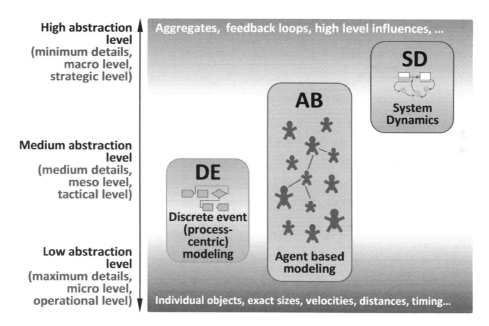

**Methods in simulation modeling**

In simulation modeling, a *method* is a general framework we use to map a real world system to its model. A method suggests a type of language, a sort of "terms and conditions" for model building. To date, there are three methods:

- *System Dynamics*

- *Discrete Event Modeling*

- *Agent Based Modeling*

Each method serves a particular range of abstraction levels. System dynamics assumes very high abstraction, and it's typically used for strategic modeling. Discrete event modeling supports medium and medium-low abstraction. In the middle are agent based models, which can vary from very detailed models where agents model physical objects to highly abstract models where the agents are competing companies or governments.

You should always select your method by carefully considering the system you want to model and your goals. In the figure below, the modeler's problem will largely determine how he models a supermarket. He could build a process flowchart where customers are entities and employees are resources, an agent based model where consumers are agents affected by ads, communication, and their interactions with agents/employees, or a feedback structure where sales are in the loop with ads, quality of service, pricing, and customer loyalty.

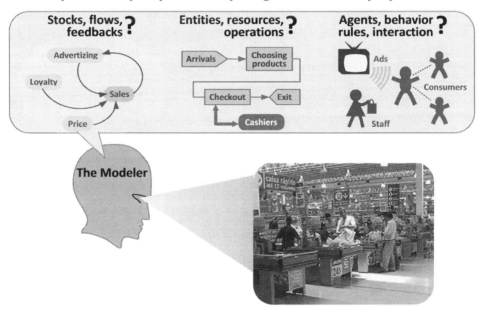

Sometimes different parts of the system are best modeled using different methods, and in these situations a multi-method model best meets your needs.

# Installing and Activating AnyLogic

AnyLogic 6 Professional's wizard-driven installation process is simple and straightforward. Download AnyLogic 6 from www.anylogic.com, and then use the following steps to install it:

1. Start AnyLogic. If it is not activated with a personal unlock key yet, the **AnyLogic Activation Wizard** will be displayed automatically.

2. On the **Activate AnyLogic** page, select **Request a time-limited Evaluation Key. The key will be sent to you by e-mail.**, and then click **Next**.

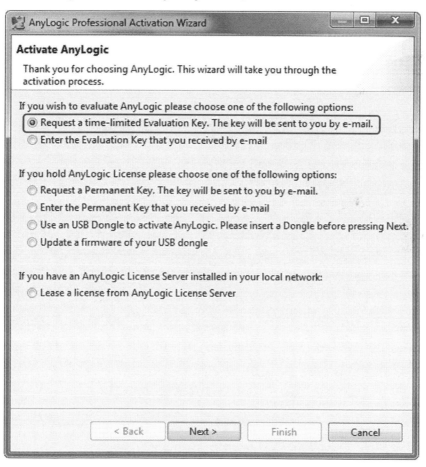

3.   On the **AnyLogic License Request** page, provide your personal information and then click **Next**.

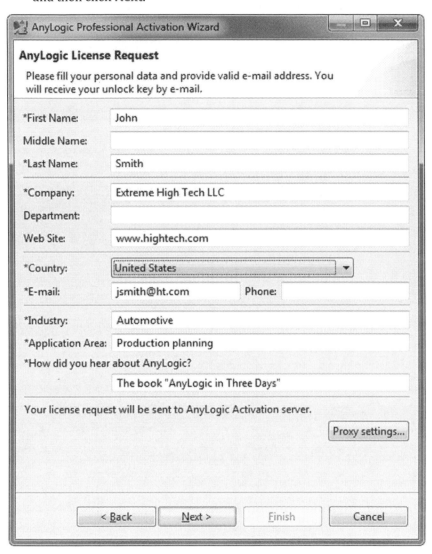

You'll receive a confirmation shortly after you send your request, and you'll receive your evaluation key in a separate e-mail.

4.  After you receive your activation key, open the AnyLogic activation wizard, select **Enter the Evaluation Key that you received by email** on the first page, and then click **Next**.

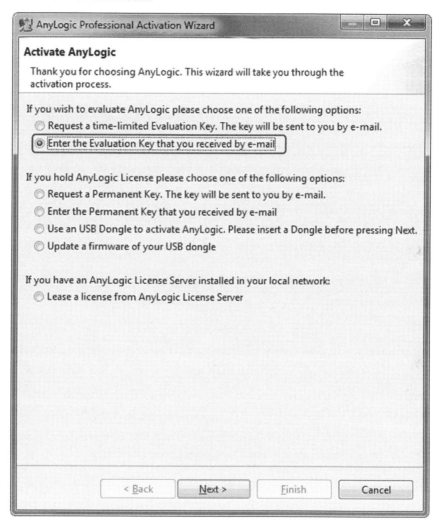

5.  Copy the received activation key from the email message you received, paste it into the **Please paste the key here** field, and then click **Next**.

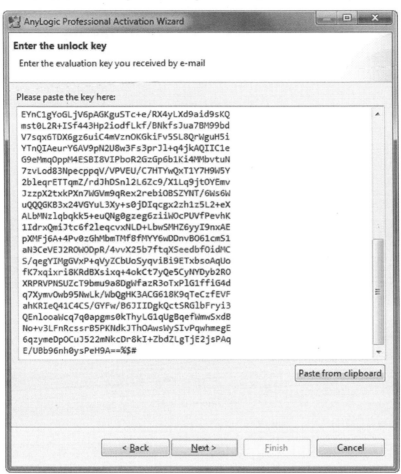

6.  You should see a message that informs you the product has been activated successfully.

7.  Click **Finish**.

You've completed AnyLogic's activation process, and you can start developing your first model.

# Discrete-event modeling with AnyLogic[1]

AnyLogic supports all three types of simulation modeling – discrete-event, agent-based and system dynamics – as well as any combination of them. In this chapter, you'll learn how to develop discrete-event models.

*Discrete event modeling* is almost as old as system dynamics. In 1961, IBM engineer Geoffrey Gordon introduced GPSS, considered the first software implementation of the discrete event modeling method. Today, a number of programs - including modern versions of GPSS - offer discrete event modeling.

> ⬥ **The idea of discrete event modeling method is this: the modeler is suggested to think about the system being modeled as of a process, i.e. a sequence of operations being performed over entities.**

The operations include delays, service by various resources, choosing the process branch, splitting, combining and some other. As long as entities compete for resources and can be delayed, queues are present in virtually all discrete event models. The model is specified graphically as a process flowchart where blocks represent operations. The flowchart usually starts with "source" blocks that generate entities and inject them into the process and ends with "sink" blocks that remove them from the model.

*Entities* (originally *transactions* in GPSS) can represent clients, patients, phone calls, physical and electronic documents, parts, products, pallets, computer transactions, vehicles, tasks, projects, and ideas. *Resources* represent staff, doctors, operators, workers, servers, CPUs, computer memory, equipment, and transport.

Service times and entity arrival times are usually stochastic, drawn from a probability distribution, thus discrete event models are stochastic themselves. This means a model must run for a certain time or requires a certain number of replications before it produces a meaningful output.

---

[1] The introduction is from "The Book of AnyLogic" (working title) being currently written by Dr. Andrei Borshchev and partially available on AnyLogic website.

Typical output expected from a discrete event model is:

- Utilization of resources
- Time spent in the system or its part by an entity
- Waiting times
- Queue lengths
- System throughput
- Bottlenecks
- Cost of the entity processing and its structure.

# Factory model

Let's first create a discrete-event model of a factory floor where washing machines are assembled from a body and a door. The parts arrive at the factory floor according to exponential distribution, and then a conveyor transfers them to an assembly station. After a robot attaches the door to the body, a conveyor transports the washing machine to the packaging line where a worker boxes it. Afterward, trucks take the completed washing machines from the factory in groups of ten.

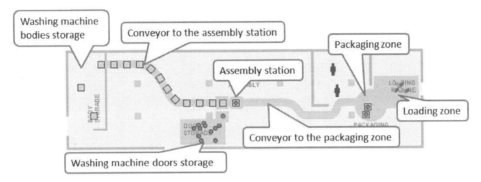

Our model development takes place across five phases, and each phase ends with a ready-to-run model.

# Phase 1. Creating a very simple model

We'll start with a very simple model to simulate how washing machine bodies enter a factory floor and how a conveyor transports them to their assembly point.

Start AnyLogic and the *Welcome* page displays.

The *Welcome page* introduces you to AnyLogic, and it provides a helpful overview of the program and its features. It also prompts you to visit XJ Technologies' website and provides access to the sample models.

1.  Close the Welcome page, and then create a new model by selecting **File|New|Model** from AnyLogic's main menu. The **New Model** wizard displays:

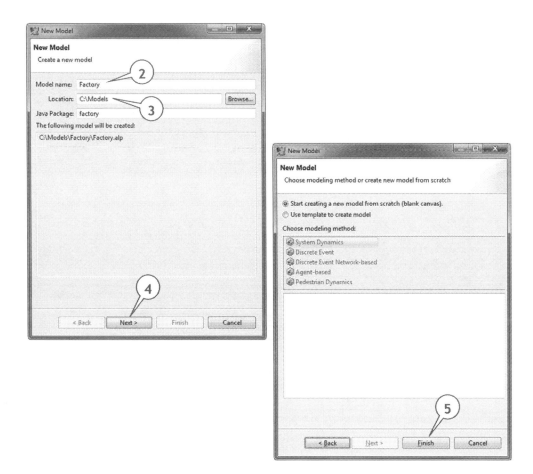

2.  In the **Model name** box, enter the new model's name: *Factory*.

3.  In the **Location** box, select the folder where you want the program to create the model. You can browse for a folder by clicking **Browse** or you can type the name of the folder you want to create in the **Location** box.

4.  Click **Next** to open the wizard's next page. You can start a model from scratch or choose a template to be your model's starting point.

5.  Since your goal is to learn how to create a model, click **Finish** to close the wizard.

In the graphical editor, you'll see the empty diagram of the model's *Main* active object class. Let's briefly introduce you to AnyLogic's interface.

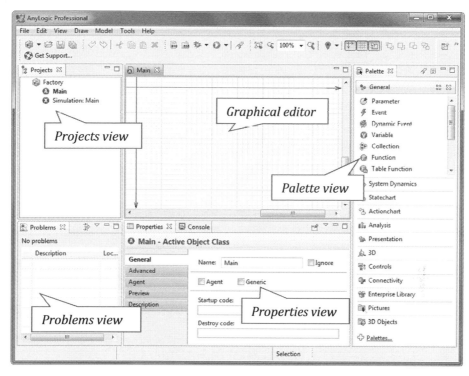

*Graphical editor*

The graphical editor allows you to graphically edit the diagram of the active object class.

*Projects view*

The **Projects** view provides access to AnyLogic models you opened in the workspace, and the workspace tree allows you to easily navigate the models.

*Palette view*

The **Palette** view lists model elements grouped in stencils (palettes). To add an element to your model, drag the element from the palette on to the graphical editor.

*Properties view*

The **Properties** view allows you to view and modify the selected item's properties.

*Problems view*

The **Problems** view displays any errors that take place as you develop and compile your model.

We'll model our factory using AnyLogic *Enterprise Library.*

## Enterprise Library

- *Enterprise Library* is AnyLogic's standard library for discrete-event or, to be more precise, process-centric modeling paradigm.

  With *Enterprise Library* objects, you can model real-world systems using *entities* (such as transactions, customers, products, parts, and vehicles), *processes* (operations sequences that typically include queues, delays, resource utilization), and *resources.*

- The processes are defined with *flowcharts* - graphical process representations used by manufacturing, call centers, business processes, logistics, and healthcare. Flowcharts are constructed from *Enterprise Library* objects.

  AnyLogic flowcharts are hierarchical, scalable, and extensible, and these properties allow you to model large and complex systems at any detail level. Another important feature of the Enterprise Library is the ability to create very sophisticated animations of process models.

6. In the **Palette** view, click the **Enterprise Library** palette to open it. You can now add library objects from the **Enterprise Library** palette to the graphical diagram of our *Main* active object class.

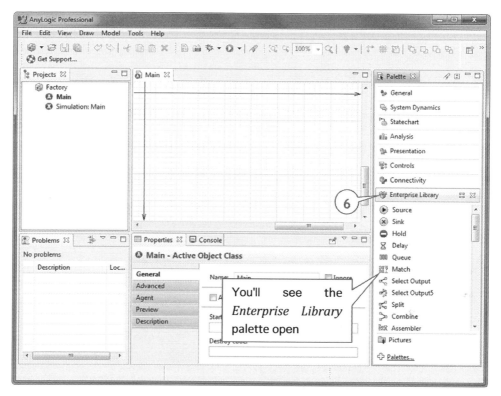

Add **Source** object to generate entities. While the **Source** object usually acts as the process model's starting point, our model will use it to generate washing machine bodies.

7. Drag the **Source** element from the **Enterprise Library** palette on to the graphical diagram. You'll find this to be the easiest and most common way to add an element to a diagram.

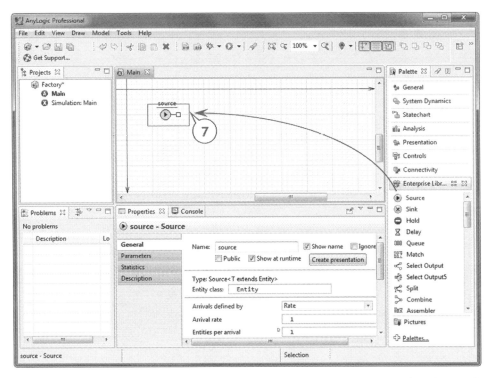

8.  After you drag an element on to the graphical editor, you'll see the element's name is selected in the in-place editor.

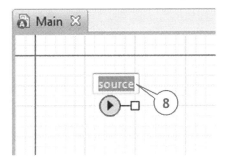

Here, you can enter the object's new name: *sourceBodies*.

🔶 **Name model elements as we do here - you'll later refer to these elements by their names.**

If you exit the in-place editor, double-click the object's name on the diagram canvas to return to editing mode.

Continue constructing the flowchart by adding more *Enterprise Library* objects:

9. Add a **Queue** object on to the diagram, and then use the in-place editor to name it *bodies*.

   The **Queue** object models a queue (a buffer) of entities waiting to be accepted by the process flow's next object or a storage of the entities. We add a queue to store the washing machine bodies until they can be placed on a conveyor.

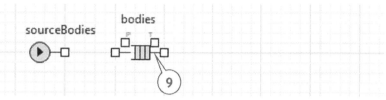

10. Add a **Conveyor** object, and then name it *conveyorBodies*.

    The **Conveyor** object moves entities along a path at a given speed, and it also ensures a minimum space separates them. In our model, the object represents a conveyor that transports washing machine bodies.

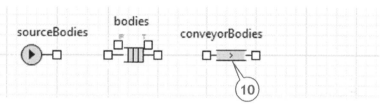

11. Add **Sink**. A **Sink** object disposes entities, and it usually acts as a flowchart's end point.

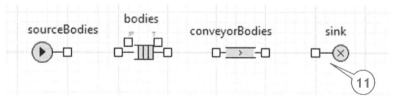

Now, we'll define a route for the entities by connecting flowchart object ports.

Connect the *sourceBodies* object's port to the *bodies* object's left port.

**12.** To connect the ports, click the port you want to connect.

**13.** Afterward, double-click another port. You'll see the connector that links these ports.

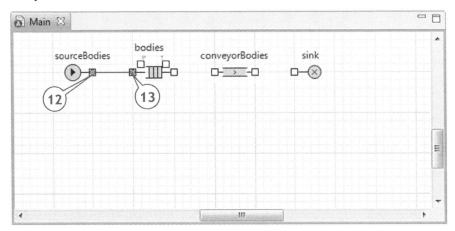

- When you draw a connector, green circles display where the connector's points are correctly placed inside a port.

- If you select a connector but you don't see a green circle, it's likely that you've placed the connector's point near the port rather than directly on it, and you need to move it there.

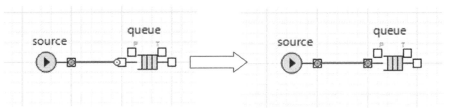

**14.** Connect ports of other flowchart objects as shown in the figure below.

In this step, you're defining the path for entities that pass through this flowchart. After an entity enters the **Source** object, the model passes it further to the flowchart object you connected to **Source** object's output port, and so forth.

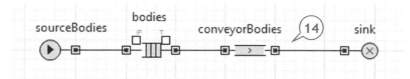

You've likely noticed you connect the object's right port to the following object's left port, and the reason is that *Enterprise Library* objects have *input* and *output* *ports*. Input ports are located on the left side of the object's icon, while output ports are on the right side. You may only connect input ports to output ports.

15. In the **Projects** view, you may see an asterisk near the model item. It means your model has unsaved changes.

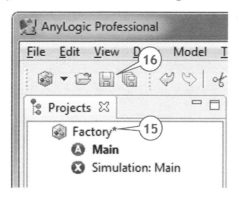

16. On the toolbar, click 🖫 **Save** to save your model.

We've finished building this very simple model, and you can now run it and watch its behavior.

17. On the toolbar, locate the **Run** button, and then click the small triangle on its right.

18. Select the experiment you want to run. Choose **Factory/Simulation** from the list.

    You can have several models open in your workspace at one time - and each model can have several experiments - so it's essential that you select the correct experiment.

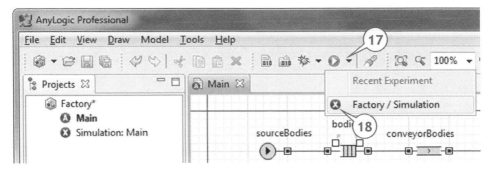

After you start the model, you'll see the presentation window that displays the presentation of the launched experiment *(Simulation)*.

By default, the experiment's presentation has the button **Run the model and switch to Main view**.

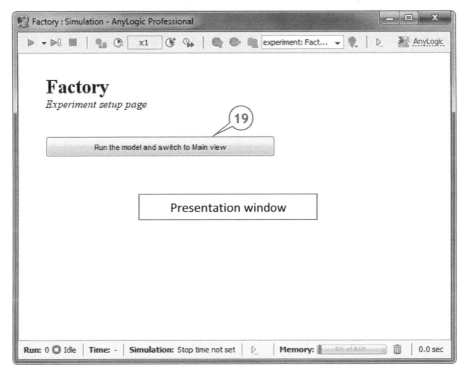

19. Click this button to run the model and open the presentation of the *Main* active object class.

You can use the animated flowchart to view the current states of your model's flowchart objects. If you look closely at the object icons, you'll notice they display statistics on entity throughput through the flowchart objects:

- The number on top of the icon shows you how many entities the object is transporting.

- The numbers near the object ports show how many entities have passed through the port.

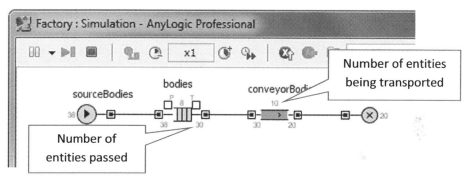

**20.** Click an object to open its inspection window.

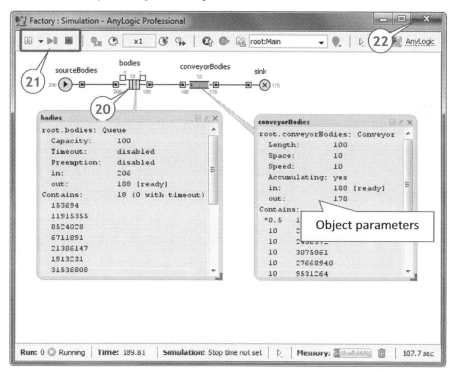

21. You can control the model execution by using the toolbar at the top of AnyLogic presentation window.

**Run from the current state**

[Visible when the model is not running] Starts the simulation or, if the simulation was paused, resumes it.

**Step**

Executes one model event, and then pauses the model execution.

**Pause**

[Visible when the model is running] Pauses the simulation. You can resume a paused simulation at any time.

**Terminate execution**

Terminates the current model execution.

22. Close the presentation window.

# Phase 2. Creating the model animation

Let's continue developing our model by adding a simple animation to represent the conveyor and the area where the factory stores washing machine bodies. We'll start by adding the factory's layout.

1.  Open the **Presentation** palette.

    The palette has *geometric shapes* for drawing model presentations such as a rectangle, a line, an oval, a polyline, a curve, and so forth.

2.  Drag the **Image** shape from the palette on to the diagram.

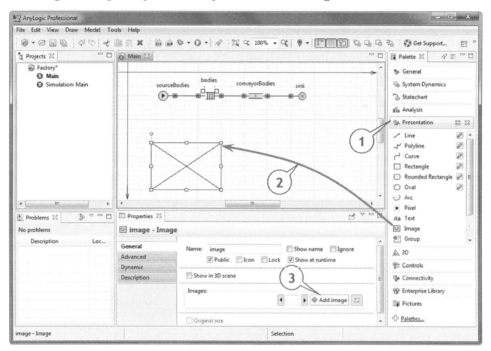

3.  Choose the image file that the image will display.

    On the **General** page of the **Properties** view, in the **Images** area, click **Add image**, and then choose the *factory_layout.png* image from AnyLogic folder*/resources/AnyLogic in 3 days/Factory* (you need AnyLogic 6.8 or later).

    In the preceding path, AnyLogic folder is the location on your computer where you've installed AnyLogic, such as *Program Files/AnyLogic 6 Professional.*

4.  On the **General** tab of the **Properties** view, select the **Original size** checkbox to use the image's original size.

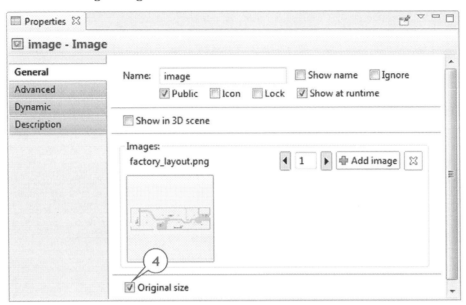

By default, AnyLogic matches the image's size to the shape's size. You can resize the image, but this can distort the image's proportions like the figure below:

Here, the picture is shown undistorted in its original size:

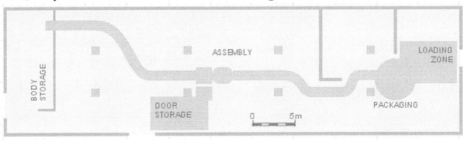

☑ Original size

5.  On the **General** page of the **Properties** view, select the **Lock** checkbox to lock the image.

By locking the image, you'll ensure you don't accidently select the image with your mouse. It will help you when you draw shapes on top of this image.

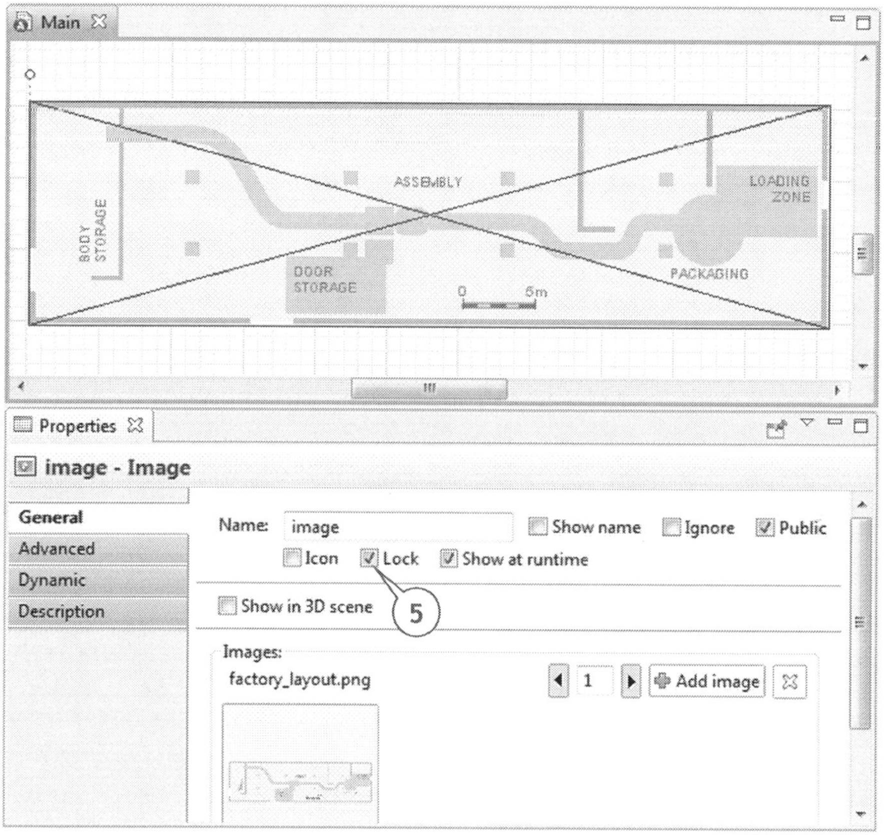

## Locking shapes

You can lock a shape to ensure it will not react to your mouse click and you will not select it in the graphical editor. It's a feature you'll find helpful when your presentation uses a background image such as a factory or hospital department's layout as a base for an animation.

In this case, you may want to edit a shape on your layout, but accidentally edit the layout instead. Sometimes it is hard to click the shape border and you may select the background image rather than the shape. By locking your background image to prevent yourself from accidently selecting the layout, you'll make drawing animations much easier.

Now, we'll draw an animation of the storage area for washing machine bodies. You'll find the corresponding area marked on the factory floor layout, and we'll draw a rectangle to match it.

6.  On the **Presentation** palette, double-click the **Rectangle** element to activate its drawing mode.

7.  Drag the rectangle over the layout's BODY STORAGE area. The rectangle will represent the area where the washing machine bodies are stored.

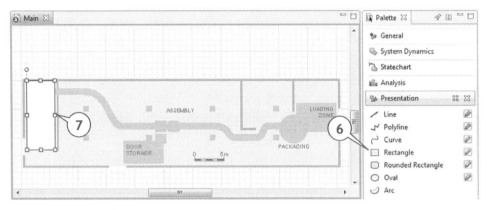

## Drawing mode

- Some elements (marked in the **Palette** with ✎ icons) support drawing mode - one more method to add elements to the diagram plus to drag'n'dropping.

- In the drawing mode, you can easily draw shapes. For example, you can draw an oval or a rectangle to match your size requirements, or you can draw a polyline point by point.

- To activate the drawing mode, double-click the element in the **Palette**. Its icon should turn to ✎. Now you can draw this shape in the graphical editor.

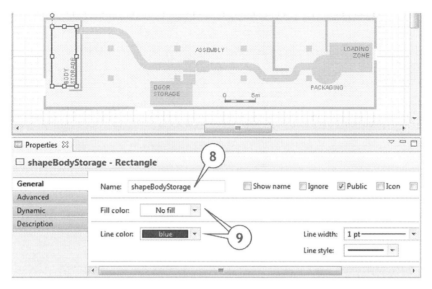

8.  In the **Properties** view, in the **Name** box, type the rectangle's name: *shapeBodyStorage*.

9.  In the **Fill color** list, click **No fill** to make the rectangle transparent, and then, in the **Line color** list, click *blue*.

## The Properties view

The **Properties** view is a context-sensitive view that displays the selected model element's properties. To modify an element's properties, select the element by clicking it in the graphical editor or in the **Projects** view, and then use the **Properties** view to modify the properties.

The **Properties** view contains several pages. To open a different page, click its tab:

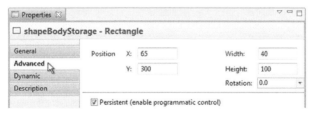

The selected element's name and the type display at the top of the view:

Now let's draw a polyline to represent a conveyor.

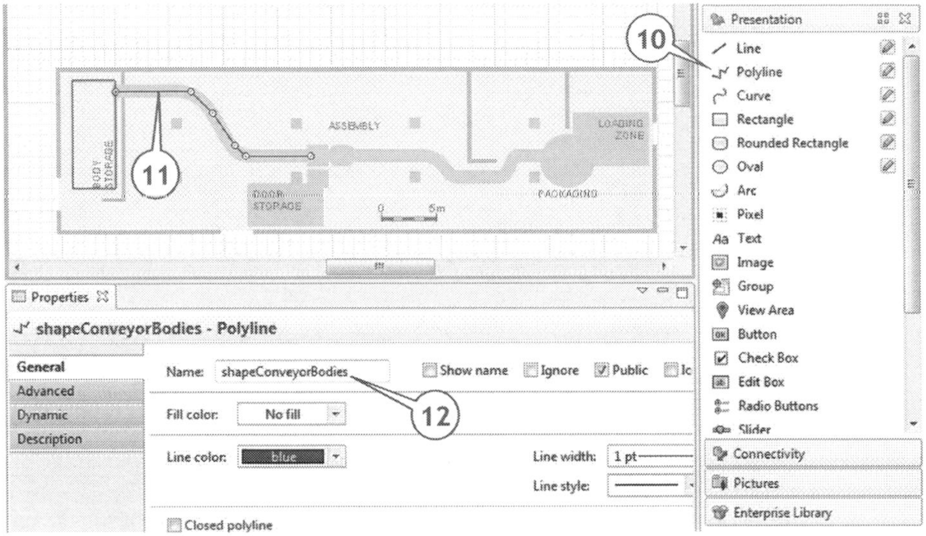

10. On the **Presentation** palette, double-click the **Polyline** element to activate its drawing mode.

11. Draw a polyline from left to right. Draw polyline points by clicking the animation and place the end polyline point by double-clicking.

12. Name the polyline *shapeConveyorBodies*. Change the **Line color** to *blue*.

## Polyline direction

When a polyline animates an Enterprise Library object such as **Queue** or **Conveyor**, it's important to correctly place the polyline's starting point. Here's why:

The **Conveyor** object transports parts from the polyline's start point to its end point.

The **Queue** object places entities in its queue from the starting point to the polyline's end point (starting point corresponds to queue's head).

When you double-click the polyline, its start point will display a small point inside its marker (in the figure below it is the left point):

Enterprise Library objects don't have built-in animations, so you should tell the object *bodies* that the rectangle *shapeBodyStorage* should be used as the shape animating the storage zone for washing machine bodies. While washing machine bodies will be in the storage zone, their animations will appear inside this rectangle.

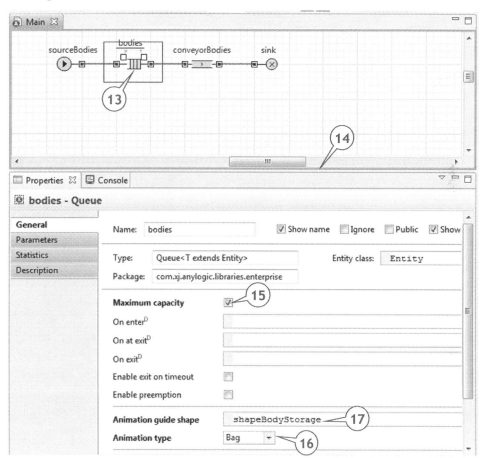

13. Select *bodies*.

Don't forget to select the object first to display its properties in the **Properties** view.

14. Enlarge the **Properties** view by dragging its border up.

15. Select the **Maximum capacity** checkbox to make the queue's capacity as large as possible.

16. Select **Bag** as **Animation type**.

17. Specify *shapeBodyStorage* as **Animation guide shape**. Type first letter "s" and press Ctrl+Space (Mac OS: Alt+space) to activate code completion assistant. Select *shapeBodyStorage* from the list.

## Code completion assistant

Use code completion assistant to avoid typing full names of variables and functions. To open the assistant, click the desired position in the edit box, and then press Ctrl+space (Alt+space on Mac OS). The popup window lists the model elements available in the given context, such as: model variables, parameters, functions, etc. Scroll to the name of the element you want to add or type the element's first letters until it appears in the list, and then press Enter to insert the name in the edit box.

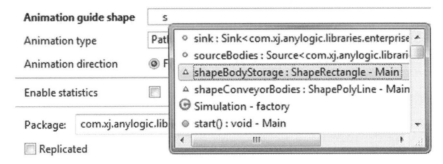

Now let's define the animation shape for our conveyor. We want to see how entitites (our washing machine bodies) move along the conveyor. The conveyor is drawn on the animation with the polyline *shapeConveyorBodies*, so:

18. Select *conveyorBodies* on the diagram and specify our polyline *shapeConveyorBodies* as its **Animation guide shape**.

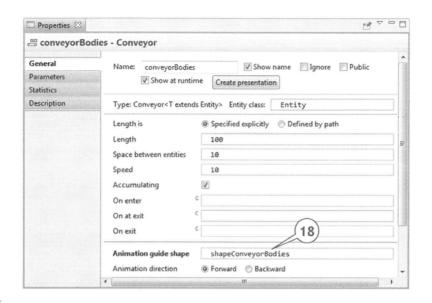

## Animation types of Enterprise Library objects

An object that performs some operation over entities (or resources) can be animated by animating entities this object handles. AnyLogic allows you to do this easily by drawing a shape on the graphical diagram—say, a polyline or a rectangle—and specifying this shape as object's **Animation guide shape**. The object then uses it as a guideline to animate the entities. There are several ways of animating entities called *animation types:*

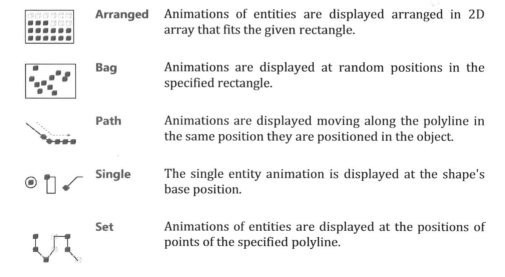

| | | |
|---|---|---|
| **Arranged** | Animations of entities are displayed arranged in 2D array that fits the given rectangle. | |
| **Bag** | Animations are displayed at random positions in the specified rectangle. | |
| **Path** | Animations are displayed moving along the polyline in the same position they are positioned in the object. | |
| **Single** | The single entity animation is displayed at the shape's base position. | |
| **Set** | Animations of entities are displayed at the positions of points of the specified polyline. | |

19. Run the model and watch its animation.

If you see the following error message, you've forgotten to choose **Bag** as the **Animation type** for the object *bodies*:

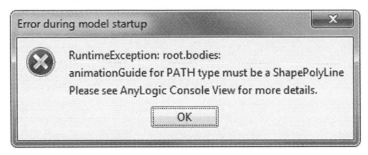

20. Look at the model animation, and you'll see washing machine bodies are stored until the conveyor transports them.

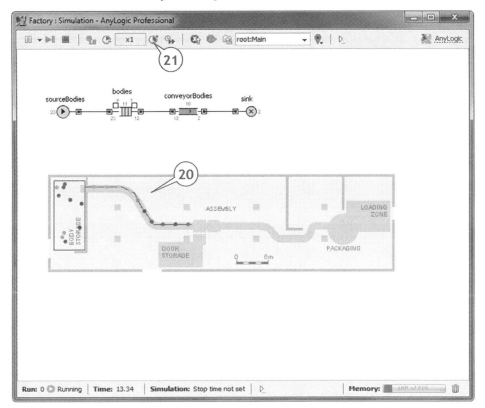

21. Adjust the model's execution speed by clicking the **Slow down** and **Speed up** toolbar buttons.

## Model execution modes

You can run an AnyLogic model in *real time* or *virtual time mode*.

- In *real time mode*, you map your model's time to real time by selecting how many model time units are equal to one second of actual time. You'll typically use real time mode when you want your animation to appear lifelike.

- In *virtual time mode*, the model runs at its maximum speed. It's useful for when you need to simulate your model for an extended period, and the model doesn't require you to define the relationship between model time units and seconds of astronomical time.

In *real time mode*, you can increase or decrease your model's execution speed by changing the model *simulation speed scale*. For example, **x2** means the model runs twice as fast as the specified model speed.

Control the model execution speed using the **Time scale** toolbar:

# Phase 3. Modeling assembly operation

In this phase, we'll do the following:

- Add a source of washing machine doors and downstream conveyor that transports them to an assembly robot.

- Add the assembly robot. The robot finishes washing machine production by attaching a door to a body.

- Modify the model animation by drawing pictures to display washing machine parts.

- Configure the flowchart objects with actual parameter values such as the conveyor's length, speed, and the space between parts.

We'll start by drawing an animation for the simulated process.

1. First, let's draw the zone of the assembly robot where washing machine bodies are placed. On the **Presentation** palette, double-click **Oval**, and then draw a circle like in the figure below:

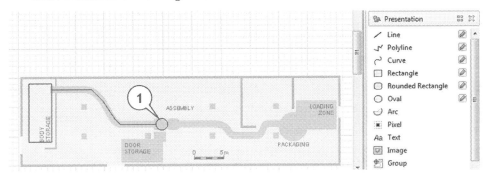

2. Name the circle *shapeBodyAtRobot*.

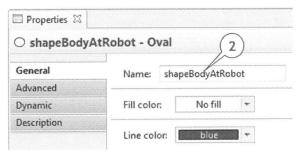

3.  Click the **Dynamic** tab of the **Properties** view.

4.  In the **Visible** box, type *false* to make this circle visible at design time and invisible at model runtime.

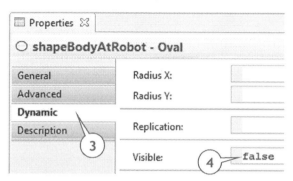

## Dynamic properties

Presentation shapes have a set of dynamic properties in addition to the static properties defined by the **General** and **Advanced** properties pages. They define the same shape properties – such as position, height, width, and color – but where static properties are treated as default values, the dynamic properties define actual values during simulation.

Dynamic properties enable animating shapes. When you define an expression in the dynamic property field, the model will reevaluate the expression on each time unit step, and then use the resulting value as the property's actual value.

If you leave the dynamic property empty, the property retains the default static value throughout the simulation.

5.  For the rectangle you drew earlier, make it invisible at runtime by clicking the **Dynamic** tab of the **Properties** view and then, in the **Visible** box, typing **false**. Afterward, repeat the same steps for the polyline you drew earlier.

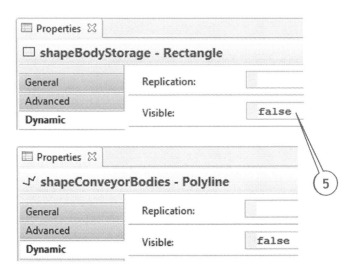

6. Draw a rectangle to represent the area where the factory stores washing machine doors when they arrive. To copy the *shapeBodyStorage* rectangle, select it and then press Ctrl (Mac OS: Cmd), drag it, and then release Ctrl (Cmd). Move the rectangle you copied to the DOOR STORAGE zone, resize it, and then name it *shapeDoorStorage*.

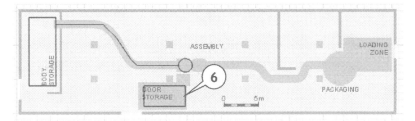

## Cloning elements

- In the graphical editor or in the **Projects** view, you can copy an element by selecting the element, pressing and holding Ctrl, and then dragging the selected element.

- Other than its name, a cloned element has the same properties as the original element.

7. Draw two circles to represent the areas where robots place doors and completed washing machines. You can draw them by cloning the circle or – if you find it difficult to clone such a small shape – by selecting the circle and then using AnyLogic's **Copy** and **Paste** commands.

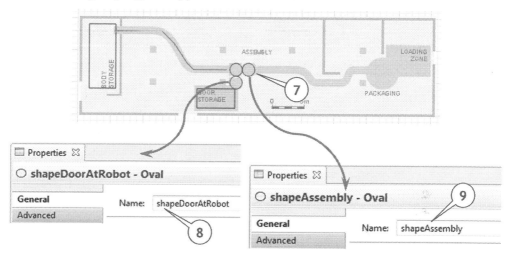

8. Name the circle *shapeDoorAtRobot*.

9. Name the right circle *shapeAssembly*.

Create a variable to define the ratio of the pixels in our presentation to the meters in our simulated physical space.

10. Drag the **Variable** from the **General** palette on to the diagram.

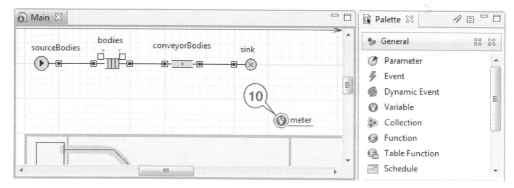

11. Name the variable *meter*.

12. Clear the **Show at runtime** checkbox to prevent AnyLogic from displaying this element on the presentation at the model runtime. The variable plays a minor role in our model, and we don't want it to be part of our presentation.

You could also use this method to hide your presentation shapes at model runtime.

13. Type *10* as the variable's **Initial value**. In our model, ten pixels will equal one meter.

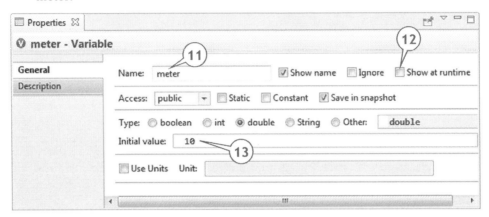

Our washing machine parts are drawn on the animation with little circles, but we want to use different images for different parts to help distinguish them. Let's draw pictures for a body, a door, and an assembled washing machine.

Entities created at the model runtime will use these shapes as their animation shapes. But until AnyLogic generates these entities, these shapes will be present on the animation where you draw them. However, we want them to be present only in the flowchart, so let's place these shapes outside the area that is shown in the model window at runtime.

A thick vertical line in the diagram denotes Y-axis, and a horizontal line denotes the X-axis. These axes separate the graphical diagram's space into four quadrants. By default, the presentation's visible part at the model runtime is the 800*600 frame in the lower-right quadrant.

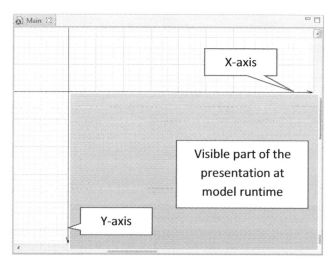

We'll draw our shapes to the left of the Y-axis so they will not be in the presentation's visible area at the model runtime.

**14.** Move the canvas a little bit to the right by right-dragging the empty area of the graphical diagram.

**15.** First, draw a rectangle to represent a washing machine body, and then name the rectangle *shapeBody*.

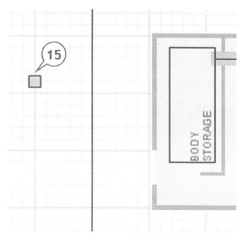

**16.** On the **Advanced** tab of the **Properties** view, use the **Width** and **Height** boxes to adjust the rectangle's size to 10x10 pixels.

Properties ⊠

☐ **shapeBody - Rectangle**

| General | Position | X: | -5 | | | Width: | 10 |
| Advanced | | Y: | -5 | | ⑯ | Height: | 10 |
| Dynamic | | | | | | Rotation: | 0.0 ▼ |
| Description | | | | | | | |

17. Draw an oval to represent a door, and then name the oval *shapeDoor*.

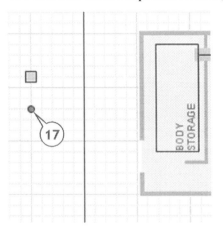

18. On the **Advanced** tab, use the **Radius X** and **Radius Y** boxes to adjust the oval's size to 3x3 pixels.

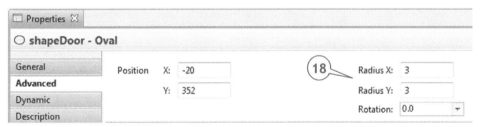

Properties ⊠

○ **shapeDoor - Oval**

| General | Position | X: | -20 | | | Radius X: | 3 |
| Advanced | | Y: | 352 | | ⑱ | Radius Y: | 3 |
| Dynamic | | | | | | Rotation: | 0.0 ▼ |
| Description | | | | | | | |

19. Now, we'll draw a picture of a washing machine. Use Ctrl+drag (Mac OS: Cmd+drag) to copy the shapes, and then place the new shapes on top of each other. In our case, place the circle on top of the rectangle, and the resulting animation should resemble the figure below:

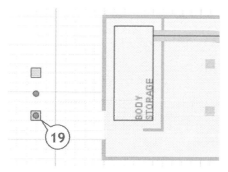

◆ **To finely position the shapes, press and hold Alt as you move them.**

Now let's create a group with a picture of an assembled washing machine.

20. Select the shape: 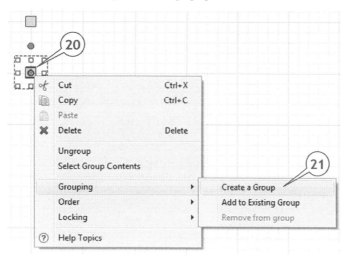 that represent the assembled washing machine.

21. Right-click (Mac OS: Ctrl+click) the selection, and then choose **Grouping | Create a Group** from the popup menu.

22. When you finish, you'll see the created group's properties. Name the group *shapeProduct.*

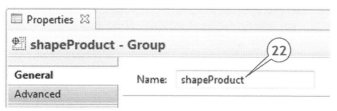

## Selecting multiple elements

You can select several elements at the same time by:

- Dragging the selection rectangle around the shapes.

- Selecting a single shape, pressing Ctrl (Mac OS: Cmd), and then holding Ctrl (Cmd) while you click other shapes to select them. To remove a shape you've selected, Ctrl+click (Mac OS: Cmd+click) the shape a second time.

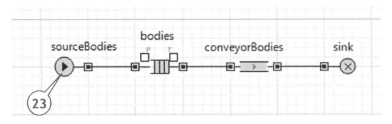

23. Modify the *sourceBodies* object's properties.

- Type *shapeBody* in the **Entity animation shape** property to set the shape that will animate washing machine bodies.

- Select the **Enable rotation** checkbox to allow you to rotate entity toward the direction in which the entity is moving.

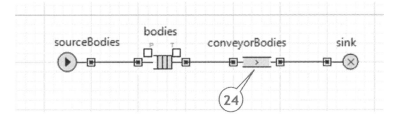

24. Modify the *conveyorBodies* object's properties.

- In the **Length is** options, select **Defined by path** to define the conveyor's length by the length of conveyor's animation shape.

- Define the minimum space between adjacent entities on the conveyor. In the **Space between entities** box, type *2\*meter*, where *meter* is the name of the variable that defines the animation pixels-to-meters ratio.

- Define the conveyor speed. In the **Speed** box, type *0.5\*meter/second()*.

## *Time functions*

AnyLogic comes with several built-in functions, and you'll find a full list in the **AnyLogic Help, AnyLogic Classes and Functions | AnyLogic functions** section. Here are some time functions you may find helpful:

- *time()* function returns the current model (logical) time.

- *second(), minute(), hour(), day(), week()* return model time values equal to one second, one minute, one hour, one day, or one week (according to the current time unit setting).

We've modified the model animation, and it's time to add details in the model logic. Add two more objects in the flowchart:

- **Source** object to model the arrival of washing machine doors.

- **Queue** object to model the storage of doors.

25. Create these objects by cloning *sourceBodies* and *bodies* objects with Ctrl+drag (Mac OS: Cmd+drag).

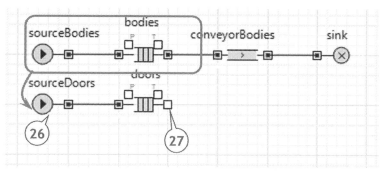

26. Name the **Source** object you created *sourceDoors*. Set *shapeDoor* as **Entity animation shape** for entities generated by this object. You can use the code completion assistant to insert the shape name.

27. Name this **Queue** object *doors* and set *shapeDoorStorage* as its **Animation guide shape**.

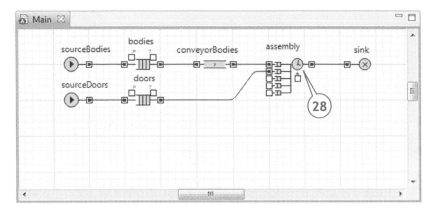

28. Add **Assembler** object and then connect it to other objects as shown on the Figure. Name it *assembly* and set the following object properties:

   - **New entity animation shape:** *shapeProduct* - use our *shapeProduct* shape to animate entities assembled by this object.

   - **Enable rotation:**  ☑  Select the checkbox to enable rotating washing machine animations towards heading when they are moving.

   - **Resource quantity:** *0* - tells the object that resources are not needed to perform the operation at the moment.

   - **Delay time:** *minute()* - set the assembly time to be equal to one minute.

   - **Animation guide shape (queue 1):** *shapeBodyAtRobot* – animation shape for the queue of washing machine bodies.

   - **Animation type (queue 1):** *Single* - one entity will be animated inside the specified animation guide shape of the first queue.

   - **Animation guide shape (queue 2):** *shapeDoorAtRobot* - animation shape for the queue of washing machine doors.

   - **Animation type (queue 2):** *Single*

   - **Animation guide shape (delay):** *shapeAssembly* – animation shape for assembly operation.

   - **Animation type (delay):** *Single*

Note that the last two options (**Animation guide shape (delay)** and **Animation type (delay)**) are at the bottom, so you'll need to scroll down the **Properties** view to find them and ensure you don't enter their values in fields with similar names (for example, in the boxes **Animation guide shape (queue3)** and **Animation type (queue 3).)**

**Assembler** object assembles one entity from the several entities that arrive at its input ports. The number of entities required to perform an assembly is specified for each port using object parameters such as **Quantity 1**, **Quantity 2**, and so forth. The object waits until each input port has the required entities, and it then produces and outputs a new entity. The assembly operation takes specified delay time. Assembly may also be performed using *resources*, a topic we'll cover later in this guide.

**29.** Run the model. You'll see the assembly process animated.

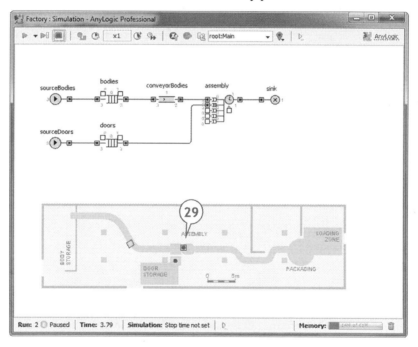

If an error message like the one below displays, you haven't set *0* as the **Resource quantity** for the *assembly*.

# Phase 4. Modeling packaging operation

Let's continue developing our model by adding logical details. We want to simulate next operations following the assembly:

- Let's add a line to pack manufactured products into boxes. Our packaging line includes the upstream conveyor and the packaging zone.

- Packed products will be placed in the loading zone, and workers will batch the boxes in groups of 10 for shipment.

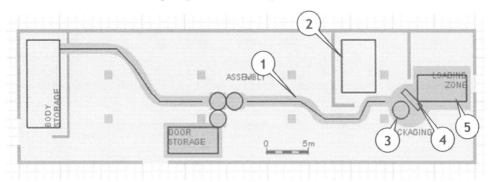

Draw five new shapes to represent the packaging zone, the packaging zone's conveyor, and the loading zone.

1. Draw the *shapeMoveToPackaging* polyline from left to right. It will represent an upstream conveyor to packaging zone.

2. Draw a rectangle to represent the workers' location, and then name it *shapeWorkers*.

3. Draw a circle *shapePrePackage* to animate the queue to packaging zone.

4. Draw a rectangle *shapePackage* to define the packaging location.

5. Draw a rectangle *shapeLoading* to define the loading zone.

Draw a picture of a box containing our washing machine.

## A set of standard pictures

The **Pictures** palette is a set of pictures of frequently-modeled objects that saves you the trouble of drawing them each time you want to add them to your presentation.

6.    Add the **Box** picture from the **Pictures** palette.

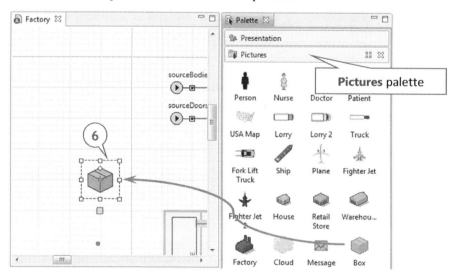

7.    In the **Name** box, name the box picture *pictureBox*.

8.  To simplify drawing small pictures, zoom in to 400%.

## Zooming the graphical diagram

AnyLogic allows you to zoom in and zoom out of a graphical diagram. To set up the diagram's scale, use the **Zoom** toolbar:

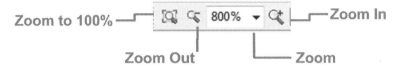

Set the required zoom by typing or selecting a value in the box, by clicking **Zoom In**, or by clicking **Zoom Out**. To return to the default zoom, click **Zoom to 100%**.

9.  Resize the picture to occupy approximately one grid cell.

10. Zoom the diagram to 100%.

Add a **Conveyor** object to model an upstream conveyor that leads to the packaging zone.

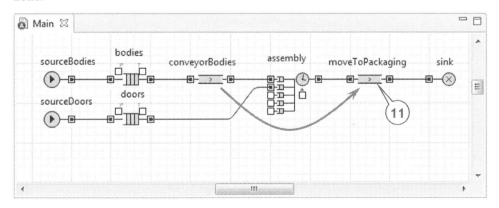

11. Add a conveyor by cloning *conveyorBodies* object. To do this, we recommend that you clone the conveyor you drew earlier – many of its parameters are already configured correctly.

12. Modify the object properties:

    - Define the **Space between entities**: *1.2\*meter.*

    - Specify the shape you'll use as the path for entity animations:
      **Animation guide shape:** *shapeMoveToPackaging.*

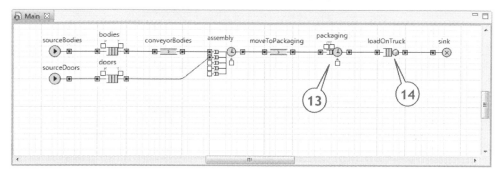

13. Add a **Service** object to model packaging a washing machine into a box. **Service** object seizes a given number of resources to perform an operation on an entity, delays the entity to model the operation, and then releases the seized resources. Modify the object properties:

    - Name the object *packaging*.

    - **Resource quantity**: *0* - We don't need resources to perform the operation.

    - Define the time needed to pack a machine into a box:
      **Delay time**: *triangular(40, 50, 120)\*second()*

    - Set up our box shape as the animation shape for the entities that exited this **Service** object:
      **On exit**: *entity.setShape(pictureBox);*

    - We assume one washing machine may wait for packaging in a prepackage zone, so we'll set the queue's capacity to 1:
      **Queue capacity**: *1*

    - Define animation shape to animate queue to packaging station:
      **Animation guide shape (queue)**: *shapePrePackage*

    - **Animation type (queue)**: *Single*

- Define animation shape to animate the packaging station itself:
  **Animation guide shape (delay):** *shapePackage*

- **Animation type (delay):** *Bag*

14. Add a **Batch** object to model loading a batch of boxes on to a truck. The **Batch** object converts several entities into one entity (*batch*) by discarding the original entities and creating a new one - a *permanent* batch - or by adding the original entities to the new entity - a *temporary* batch that can be later unbatched by an **Unbatch** object.

- Name it *loadOnTruck*.

- Define where to draw packed washing machines:
  **Animation guide shape:** *shapeLoading*

- **Animation type:** *Bag*

## Parameters of library objects: static, dynamic and code

AnyLogic library objects (**Enterprise Library**, **Pedestrian Library**, **Rail Library** and **Road Traffic Library**) have parameters of three types:

- *Static.* Evaluated once, but may be changed during the model execution. You can use a static parameter's field to define its value (that can be casted to the parameter type).

- *Dynamic.* Evaluated each time it is needed, e.g. each time the delay time, the speed or other property of an entity needs to be obtained.

- *Code.* Dynamically executed code piece that is evaluated each time a certain event occurs at the object: the entity enters or exits it, conveyor stops, etc. Here, you should place a semicolon after each line of code.

| Parameter type | Object | Parameter | Example |
|---|---|---|---|
| **Static** | *Queue* | *Capacity* | *15* |
| **Dynamic** | *Delay* | *Delay time* | *uniform(2,entity.complexity\*60)* |
| **Code** | *Sink* | *On enter* | *dataset.add( time() - entity.timestamp );* <br> *serviced++;* |

## *Distinguishing parameters of different types*

- In the **Properties** view, *dynamic* parameters have a small D icon after their names.

- *Code* parameters have C icon.

- *Static* parameters don't have an icon.

In *Library Reference Guides*, dynamic and code parameters have a *[dynamic]* label. For the code parameters, they have a *void* type (see the parameter description's **Syntax:** line) and their names typically start with **On....**

15. Run the model. You'll see how products are packed into boxes and how batches of boxes are shipped from the factory.

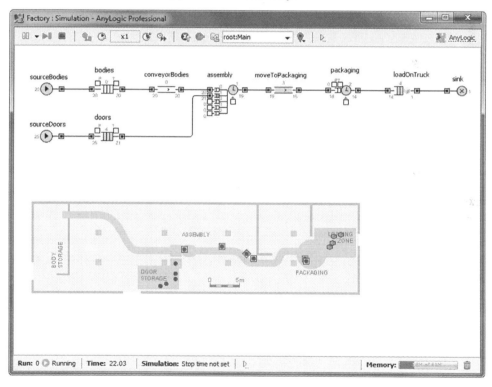

## Fixing runtime errors

Run the model several times in the virtual time mode, and you'll see the following message. It tells us the model has a bottleneck - a logical error with the system.

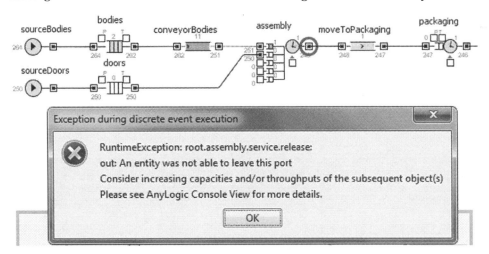

The message's first line has information about the model element that caused the error. Here, it's the *assembly* object of the *root* (in this case, *root* is the name of the main active object class, instance of *Main* class created on the model startup). The second line describes the error - an entity could not leave the object's output port, and the animated flowchart highlights the port in red.

In our case, the entity was ready to leave the assembly and it could not wait inside the object's output port. However, the succeeding *moveToPackaging* conveyor had another entity being placed at the entry of this conveyor, and the bottleneck took place when there was nowhere to put there one more entity.

The third line suggests how you can solve the problem: increase capacities or add a buffering object. You can solve the problem by adding a **Queue** object between the *assembly* and the *moveToPackaging* conveyor.

# Phase 5. Adding resources

Assembly and packaging operations need resources – an assembly robot and packagers. In this phase we'll:

- Add two types of resources: one robot to assemble the washing machines and two workers to package them.

- Collect utilization statistics for our workers and use a bar chart to display them.

- Introduce assembly robot downtime.

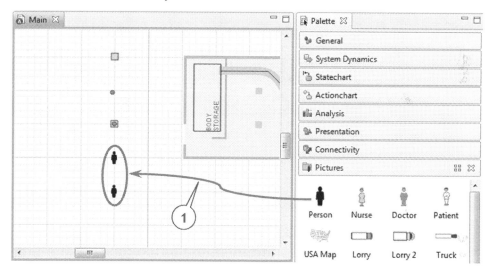

1. Draw two pictures to denote idle and busy workers.

   Rather than use primitive shapes such as rectangles or polylines, you can take the corresponding picture from the **Pictures** palette. Drag the **Person** picture from the **Pictures** palette on to the diagram two times.

   Let's change colors of our pictures.

## *Customizing standard pictures*

AnyLogic pictures are actually usual groups made from common AnyLogic presentation shapes. They allow you to adjust the picture's appearance by editing the shapes' visual properties such as their color and size.

In our case, we'll change the person picture's color by changing the fill color of the curve used to draw this picture.

2.    Click the picture. The first click selects the group.

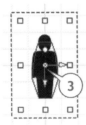

3.    The next click selects the shape - member of the group. You'll see the origin of group coordinates and the shape properties.

4.    Change the shape's **Fill color**.

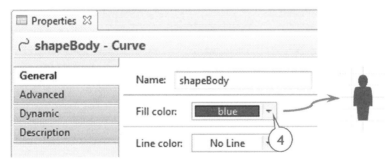

5.    Change another picture's color to red, and then rename the blue picture to *shapeWorkerIdle* and the red picture to *shapeWorkerBusy*.

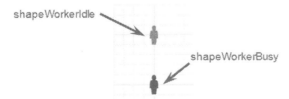

Let's add two types of resources – one to represent robots and the other to represent workers.

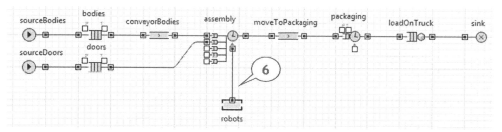

6.  Add **ResourcePool** object to model robot. The **ResourcePool** object defines a set of resources - the objects that entities use to perform their operations. Entities use **Seize, Release, Service** and **Assembler** objects to seize and release objects.

    ●  Name the object *robots*.

    ●  Connect the **ResourcePool** object's port to the *assembly* object's lower port as shown.

7.  Open the *assembly* object's properties, and then define the resource quantity: **Resource quantity**: *1*.

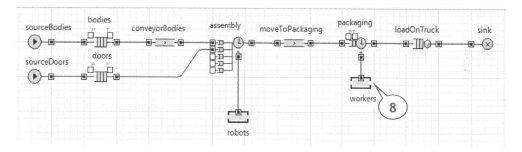

8.  Add another **ResourcePool** object to model packagers, connect its port to the *packaging* object's lower port, and then modify the object's properties:

    ●  Name this object *workers*.

    ●  Define the number of available resources:
       **Capacity**: *2*.

    ●  Resource units can be idle or busy, and you can associate different animations with these states. Set *shapeWorkerBusy* and *shapeWorkerIdle* shapes workers to denote busy and idle workers:

> **Idle unit animation shape:** *shapeWorkerIdle*
> **Busy unit animation shape:** *shapeWorkerBusy*

- Choose the *shapeWorkers* rectangle as the workers' location:
  **Animation guide shape:** *shapeWorkers*.

- Select the **Enable statistics** checkbox to allow this object to collect resource utilization statistics.

9. Go to the *packaging* object's properties, and then define the number of resources the packaging operation requires: **Resource quantity:** *1*.

Add a chart to display packagers' utilization statistics - mean percent of busy workers.

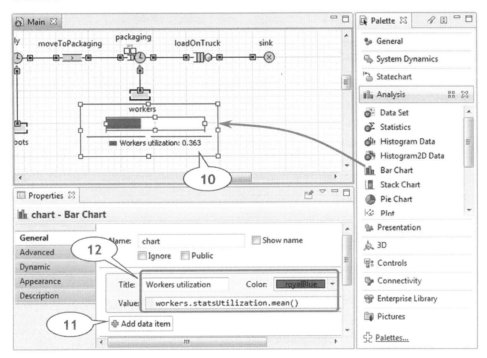

10. Open the **Analysis** palette, and then drag the **Bar Chart** on to the diagram.

The **Analysis** palette has elements that store simulation output and calculate statistics (**data set, statistics,** etc.) and several charts (**bar chart, stack chart, time plot, histogram,** etc.) for visualizing the data.

11. Click **Add data item** to add the statistics you want to draw on the chart.

12. Modify the data item's properties:

- **Title:** *Workers utilization* – the data item's title.

- **Value:** *workers.statsUtilization.mean()*

  *workers* is our **ResourcePool** object's name, *statsUtilization()* is the function that collects resource utilization statistics, and *mean()* returns the mean of the statistics it collects.

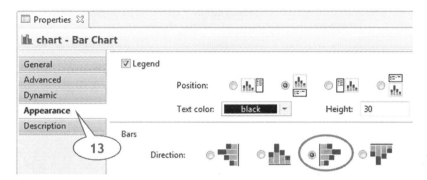

13. Adjust the chart's appearance by opening the **Appearance** properties tab and then, in the **Bars** area, selecting the **Direction** option.

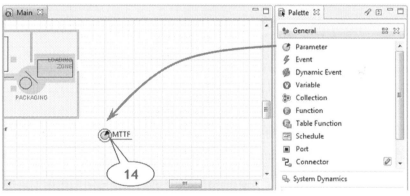

14. Add a parameter to define the mean time before robot failure. Drag the **Parameter** from the **General** palette on to the diagram. Name it *MTTF* (stands for Mean Time To Failure). Define the parameter's **Default value:** *45\*day()* – here we use AnyLogic function *day()* to get value equal to one day.

15. Add another parameter - *MTTR* (Mean Time To Repair) - to define the mean time to repair the robot, and then define the parameter's **Default value:** *7\*day()*

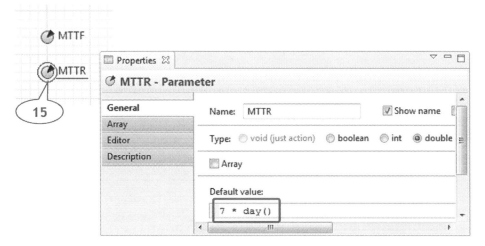

Define the robot behavior using a *statechart*.

## Statecharts

- The best way to define a behavior is to use a *statechart*. The statechart's states are alternative: the object can only be in one state at a time.

- An active object may have multiple statecharts, but now we need only one.

- *Statechart* is the most advanced construct to describe event- and time-driven behavior. For some objects, this event- and time-ordering of operations is so pervasive that you can best characterize their behavior using a state transition diagram – a statechart.

- *Statechart* has *states* and *transitions*. *Transitions* may be triggered by user-defined conditions (timeouts or rates, messages received by the statechart, and Boolean conditions). *Transition* execution may lead to a state change where a new set of transitions becomes active. *States* in the statechart may be hierarchical, i.e. contain other states and transitions.

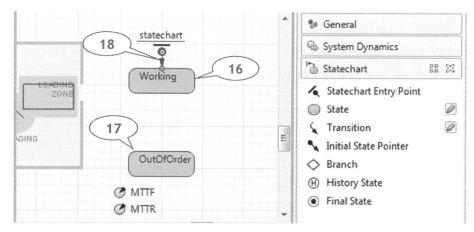

16. Start drawing a statechart by drawing two states. Drag a **State** from the **Statechart** palette on to the diagram, and then name it *Working*.

17. Add another state below, and then name it *OutOfOrder*.

18. Add a **Statechart entry point** pointing to *Working* state. The statechart entry point's name is the statechart's name. Make sure you've connected its end point to a state (select the pointer – the connected point should be indicated with green as shown).

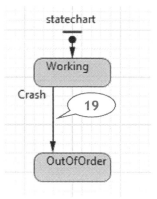

19. Draw a transition from *Working* to *OutOfOrder* state to model robot failure. To do so, double-click the **Statechart** palette's **Transition** element, click *Working* state, and then click *OutOfOrder*.

20. Name the transition *Crash*.

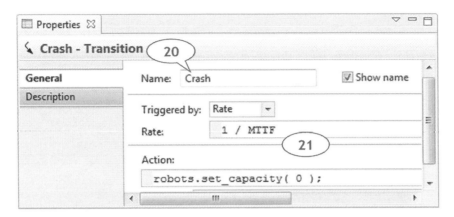

21. Set it up to trigger with time exponentially distributed with the mean of *MTTF* (45 days):

    - **Triggered by**: *Rate* – means exponential distribution with mean **Rate**.

    - **Rate**: *1/MTTF*

    - **Action**: *robots.set_capacity( 0 )* – this method of **ResourcePool** object sets the resource's capacity to zero. If the resource's capacity is zero, the *assembly* object will not assemble washing machines because there are no available resources.

22. Draw a transition from *OutOfOrder* to *Working* state.

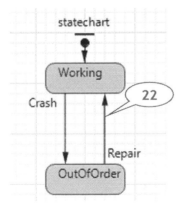

23. Name the transition *Repair*.

24. This transition will model the robot recovery. Set this transition to take place with a mean of *MTTR* (7 days):

- **Triggered by:** *Rate* – means exponential distribution with mean **Rate**.

- **Rate:** *1/MTTR*

- **Action:** *robots.set_capacity( 1 )*

## Modifying static parameters at runtime

- You can modify a library object's static parameters dynamically at model runtime.

- To change a parameter's value, call the automatically generated method *set_parameterCodeName()*, passing the value you want to assign as a method parameter.

  For example, to change the **Capacity** of *queue* object to *50*, call *queue.set_capacity(50);*

- To find a parameter's programmatic name, refer to *Library Reference Guide* for full descriptions of the object parameters.

  For example, to find the code name for **Source**'s **Arrival rate**, open the **Source** object's help document, and then search for **Arrival rate** section. You'll find the required name in the **Syntax:** row.

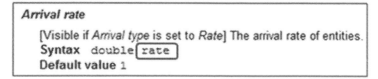

Now we've finished creating our first factory model.

25. Run the model and increase the model execution speed to run the simulation faster.

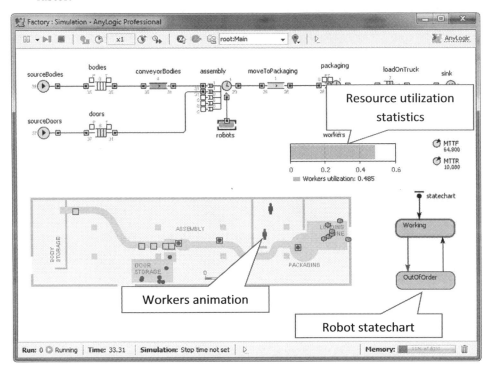

You can now analyze how equipment downtime and the resulting maintenance period affect the factory's performance.

# Network-based modeling

We've built a discrete event manufacturing model of the factory where we abstracted from exact physical trajectories and used average timings. We've also created the process flowchart and defined timings for the factory's operations.

However, some processes take place in a physical space with moving entities and resources. As an example, let's assume we want to model a hospital department to find a work schedule for doctors and nurses that meets a required service quality level.

While this model also uses schedules and timings, we need to consider how patients, nurses, and doctors move within the department. Rather than define a travel time for each possible route, we can define a speed for the model's entities and resources, draw a network of nodes and segments on the department layout, define the process logic using a flowchart and place entities (patients) and resources (doctors and nurses) in the network. Afterward, patients will use the shortest path to move between rooms.

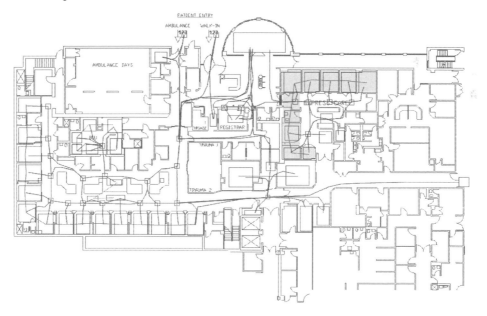

**The Trauma Center model's network definition**

The approach that involves drawing a transportation network for entities and resources on a layout of simulated physical space is network- or layout-based modeling.

Network based modeling is successfully used in complex service, logistics, and healthcare systems where layout is important and there is a network of locations and paths between them which entities use as routes (and route lengths matter).

Another example of a network-based model is a transportation network in a logistics model. Here, the entities are trains that transfer the cargo, network nodes stand for terminals, and railways are defined with network segments.

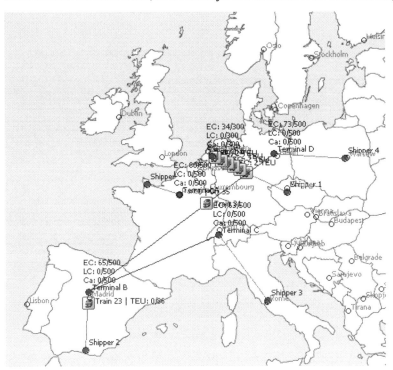

**Network-based model of a terminal network**

# Retailer Model

Let's build a model of a retailer warehouse. For simplicity, we'll assume this store sells just one product.

The retailer works as follows:

- The retailer orders a number of products. When the retailer receives them, they store the products in their warehouse.

- Products are regularly sold by the store. When a new request for a product arrives, a product is removed from storage and sold to the customer.

- When the number of stored products reaches a set level, the retailer orders additional products to increase the inventory.

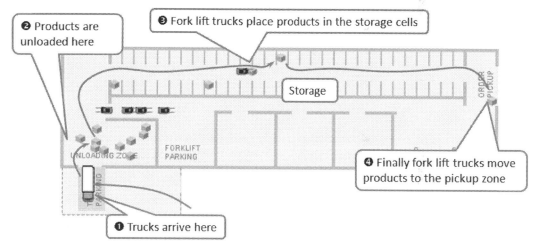

## *Warehouse Operations and Layout Optimization*

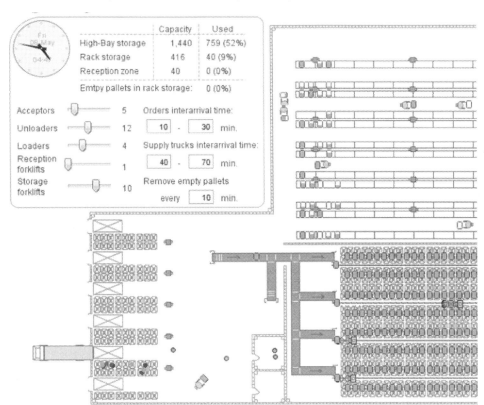

### High-Bay Warehouse model

Constructing and fitting out a modern warehouse – with all its required equipment and tools – is an expensive undertaking. The planning and design stages are key, and mistakes can reduce warehouse utility and performance and increase operational costs. You should also pay careful attention to operational optimization; increased loads can affect the performance of a warehouse which once operated effectively.

Simulation modeling is the modern tool that makes it easier to design, layout, and optimize warehouse operations. Simulating a warehouse implies developing a computer model and testing it by executing computational experiments with combinations of parameters based on that model these experiments provide a low-cost and low risk method to determine the optimal parameter set for a warehouse under development or redesign.

The first step in creating a model is to detail the warehouse's structure: the exact location of major zones and transportation routes. Afterward, we'll specify the business processes the warehouse uses to operate: the who, what, and when of resources (staff and equipment) associated with various procedures. We consider material arrival schedules, including variables such as parts, volume, and timing. During model operation, we typically collect detailed warehouse operations statistics such as resource utilization rates, activity durations, and completion times.

Warehouse modeling deliverables often include items such as a detailed report that describes the warehouse's design, suggested changes to lay out a stone optimization results, software caught allowing the customer to reach these determinations himself, or an ongoing software decision support system. Whatever the deliverable, most warehouse simulation solutions address:

- the required quantity and type of transportation and material handling equipment
- staff level requirements
- floor space requirements and layout
- ultimate scenarios of equipment lay out an arrangement
- calculating performance metrics such as execution time
- resource utilization rates, inventory levels, etc.
- calculating and optimizing warehouse operational expenses
- determining the optimal number of loading and unloading gates
- developing more effective freight traffic flows
- optimizing operational timetables

# Phase 1. Network and storage modeling

We'll start with a very simple model that will use the following assumptions:

- The retailer receives an average of one item per minute, and places delivered products into the unloading zone.

- When the retailer receives a product, a forklift truck brings it to one of the warehouse's empty storage cells.

- The product spends an average of 20 to 45 minutes in the storage cell until another forklift removes it.

1.  Create a new model, and then name it *Retailer*.

Add the layout of the retailer's warehouse. Adding a layout and then drawing a transportation network over it is the first step in building a network based model.

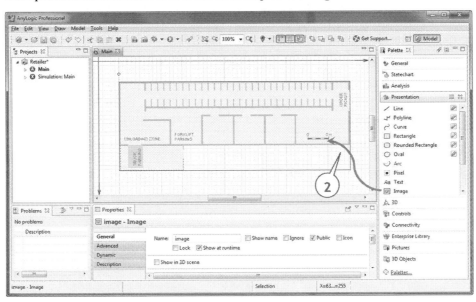

2.  Drag the **Image** from the **Presentation** palette on to the diagram.

3.  Choose the image file that the image will display. On the **Properties** view, on the **General** tab, click **Add image**, and then choose the *retailer_layout.png* image from AnyLogic folder*/resources/AnyLogic in 3 days/Retailer*.

4.  Select the **Lock** checkbox to lock the image shape.

5.  Select the **Original size** checkbox.

Use AnyLogic's shapes to define important areas and routes on top of the layout. AnyLogic will use your animation to generate the network's logical structure.

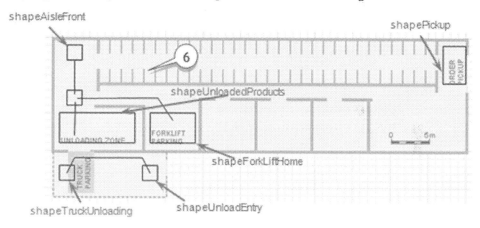

6. Draw locations with rectangles. Make them transparent by choosing **No color** in the **Fill color** property and optionally change the **Line color** to *blue*. Give the rectangles the same names as the rectangles in the picture - we'll later refer to these shapes by their names. Draw an intermediate node (its name doesn't matter, and it is not shown on the figure). Connect rectangles with polylines. These polylines will act as paths for entities moving in our model (trucks and fork lift trucks).

## Drawing a network

- A network is made of nodes and segments. Nodes define where entities and resources can stay during the simulation, while segments connect nodes and serve as paths for moving entities and resources.

- Network nodes are defined with rectangles.

- Network segments can be drawn with lines or polylines.

- There are some certain connection rules you should know:

- One polyline can connect several nodes, but you should point a salient point of a polyline into each rectangle you want to. In the figure below the polyline has three points and connects the three nodes:

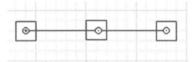

- If a polyline does over some rectangle but doesn't have a salient point inside it, this node is not connected. And in case it is not connected with some other network segment, it doesn't get into the network. In the figure below, the polyline doesn't have a salient point inside the middle node and connects only the leftmost and the rightmost nodes:

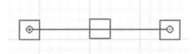

7.  Add the drawn shapes to a group.

Select all of the drawn shapes by dragging your mouse over the area with the shapes. You can also right-click (Mac OS: Ctrl+click) the diagram and then choose **Select All** from the popup menu to select the unlocked elements.

After you select the shapes, right-click (Mac OS: Ctrl+click) them, choose **Grouping | Create a group** from the popup menu, and then name the group *networkGroup*.

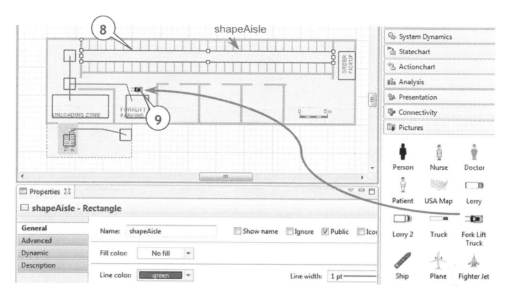

8.  Draw a rectangle to define the storage aisle's shape, and then name it *shapeAisle.* You *should not* add this shape to the group with our network shapes.

9.  Add a picture of a fork lift truck by dragging the **Fork Lift Truck** element from the **Pictures** palette on to the diagram.

Now, we'll draw an animation of a box with our product, and we'll avoid recreating it by reusing the element we created.

10. We have drawn it earlier in *Factory* model, so you can find it (*pictureBox* element) by expanding the **Presentation** branch of the *Main* of *Factory* model in the **Projects** tree. Copy it to *Main* inside the *Retailer* model using the context menu's copy and paste commands.

One more thing we need to copy here from our *Factory* model - the variable that defines the relationship between a distance within our simulated space (in meters) and our animation (in pixels).

11. Expand the **Variables** branch of *Main* class of *Factory* model and copy the variable *meter* to *Main* inside the *Retailer* model.

Add the specified **Enterprise Library** objects on to the *Retailer* diagram and then modify their properties:

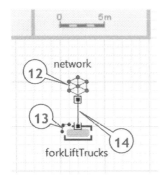

12. Add **Network** object. **Network** object maintains the network topology, defines its parameters, and manages network resources. Go to the object properties and specify **Group of network shapes**: *networkGroup*. Here, *networkGroup* is the name of the group with rectangles and polylines that defines the network structure.

13. Add **NetworkResourcePool** object to define a set of network resource units. In our case, the object represents fork lift trucks.

    • Name the object *forkLiftTrucks*.

    • In the **Capacity** field, define the number of resources of this type: *5*.

    • Specify the **Speed** at which the resources will move: *1\*meter/second()*.

    • Specify the shape that will animate these resources. Type *fork* in the **Idle unit animation shape** and **Busy unit animation shape** boxes (*fork* is the name of our picture of a fork lift truck).

    • Select the **Enable rotation** checkbox to enable rotating resource animation towards heading when the unit is moving.

    • Define the home location for these resources. In the **Home node** field, type the name of the rectangle that defines the corresponding network node: *shapeForkLiftHome*.

14. Connect these objects to tell resources they will operate in the network defined by this **Network** object. The association with a particular network is made by connecting the **NetworkResourcePool** object's port to the **Network** object's port.

A group of **Enterprise Library** objects with the common **Network** prefix is for network or layout-based modeling. You can easily distinguish them by their blue icons.

## Network resources

There are three types of resources associated with a network: static, moving, and portable.

- *Static* resources are bound to a particular network location (i.e. node), and they can't move or be moved. An example of a static resource would be an X-ray room or a weigh bridge.

- *Moving* resources can move on their own, and they can represent staff, vehicles, etc.

- *Portable* resources can be moved by entities or by moving resources. A portable U-Sound device or a wheelchair would be an example.

Moving and portable resources have their home locations where they can optionally return or be returned.

Entity can seize one or several units, release units, send seized units to a particular location, attach units so that they will move with the entity, and detach attached units.

Run the model to ensure there are no errors. Afterward, you should see a picture similar to the one below with five fork lift trucks in the forklift parking zone.

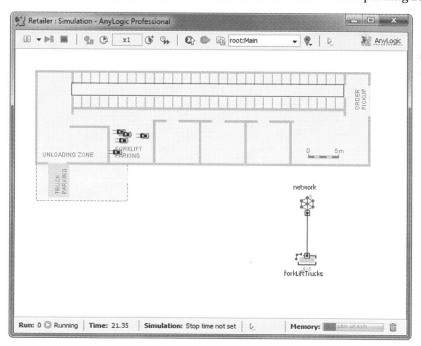

## Fixing mistyping errors

A common error you may encounter as you build your models is a misnamed model element. Names in AnyLogic are case-sensitive, which means the shape *shapeForkLiftHome* and *shapeforklifthome* typed in the property of a different object will cause the following error:

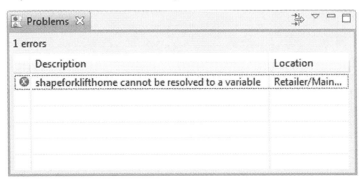

To fix an error, double-click it in the **Problems** view. If the error is graphical, AnyLogic will highlight the element that caused the error in the graphical editor. If the error is in an element's property, AnyLogic will open the element's properties and will focus in the field where the problem occurred. Try to understand the reason for the problem and fix it.

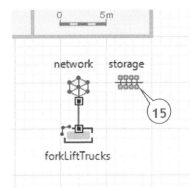

15. Add **NetworkStorage** object to model warehouse storage, and then modify the object's properties:

   - **Name:** *storage*
     **Network:** *network*
     **Positions (per row):** *30* - our storage will have 30 cells in a row. The parameter **Positions (per row)** defines how many network nodes will be

created on each side of the aisle; each node is actually a footprint of several vertical cells (controlled by **Number of levels** parameter).

- Therefore, a storage with 60 positions and 4 levels will have 60 * 4 * 2 = 480 cells, 2 means the two rows on each side of the aisle. Each cell has three coordinates: row (0..1), position (0..npositions), and level (0..n levels).

  **Shape of the aisle:** *shapeAisle*

  **Position depth:** *15*

  **Front end entry node:** *shapeAisleFront*

  **Back end entry node:** *shapePickup*

  **Draw stored entities:** *At the center of the cell*

## Modeling warehouse storages

A set of four Enterprise Library objects simplifies modeling of storages with multiple locations and regular structure, such as warehouse storages.

**NetworkStorage** defines a storage of cells. Each cell may store one entity at a time. **NetworkStorage** object models two opposite racks and an aisle between them. It creates a set of nodes and segments along a given aisle, adds them to a network, and manages the entities in the locations on both sides of the aisle.

You'll need to draw three rectangles to define the storage: **Front end entry node** (in our case - *shapeAisleFront*), **Shape of the aisle** *(shapeAisle)*, and **Back end entry node** *(shapePickup)*. Both entry nodes must belong to the network, but the aisle shape does not.

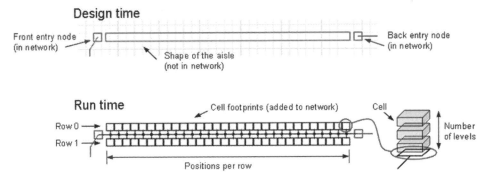

A network path is created from the front entry node through the aisle's center axis to the back entry node. Between each pair of opposite cell nodes, **NetworkStorage** creates a short path across the aisle and a small node in the aisle's center so that all cell nodes are connected to the network.

The width of the cell footprint nodes (i.e. their dimension along the row) is calculated automatically as the length of the aisle divided by the number of positions per row. Create a flowchart from **Enterprise Library** objects as shown on the picture below. Name the objects like shown in the figure.

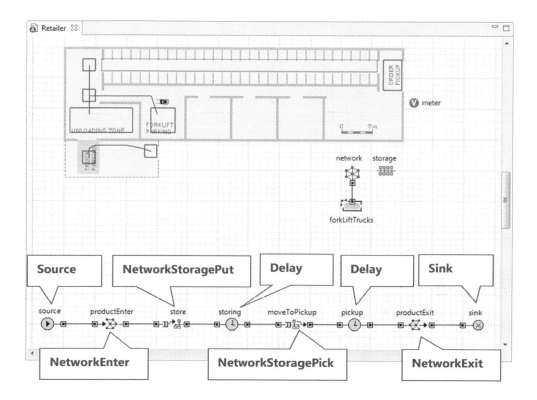

You can see that the **Network...** objects can be easily mixed with regular process objects like **Delay, Queue**, etc.

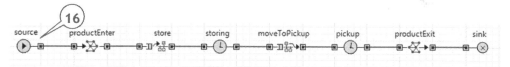

16. **Source** object models products arrivals to our retailer.

   • Specify our shape *pictureBox* in the **Entity animation shape** property of the object. This shape will animate entities generated by this **Source** object.

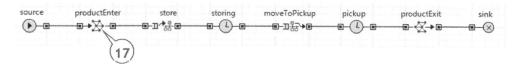

17. **NetworkEnter** object adds incoming entity into the network and then places it at the specified network node.

- The **Network** parameter defines the network the entity will enter. Here, type our **Network** object's name: *network*.

- In the **Entry node** field, you define the network node where the entity will appear. Here, you must type the name of the rectangle that defines the corresponding node: *shapeUnloadedProducts.*

- Specify the **Speed** at which the entity will move in the network. Typing here *forkLiftTrucks.speed* we set speed the same as that of the fork lift trucks.

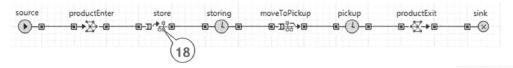

18. **NetworkStoragePut** puts an entity (optionally with the help of moving resources) into a cell of a given storage or a storage zone. The entity is moved from its current location to the cell location. This **NetworkStoragePut** object models how incoming products are placed into the warehouse storage.

- Define the storage where the model places the entity. Type *storage* (the name of our **NetworkStorage** object) in the **Storage or zone** parameter.

- Select the **Use resources to move** checkbox since we want products to be brought to warehouse cells by resources - fork lift trucks.

- Tell the object what resources should be used to transport products to the storage. To do this, specify the list of names of **NetworkResourcePool** objects defining the required resources in the **List of resources {pool1, ...}** parameter, type *{forkLiftTrucks}* here.

You should place the resource list - even if it has only one element - in curly brackets.

Any time an operation takes place across multiple resource units, the list of their **NetworkResourcePool** objects is specified. For example, you should write *{ Nurse, Nurse, XRay }* to seize two nurses and an x-ray room.

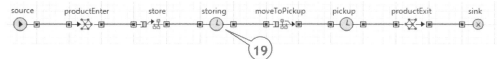

19. **Delay** object delays entities for a set time. We use it to model storing products in the warehouse storage.

    - Define the storage time in the **Delay time** field: *uniform(20, 45)* * *minute()*

    - Select the **Maximum capacity** checkbox to make the object's capacity as large as possible. We'll need this capacity to allow our object to delay an unlimited number of entities at the same time.

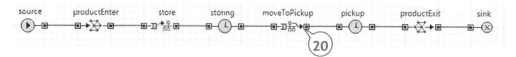

20. **NetworkStoragePick** object removes an entity from a storage cell and then moves it to the specified destination location. This is optionally done with the help of moving resources. We add it to model how a fork lift truck extracts a product from its storage cell.

    - Define the **Storage or zone** where the entity is currently stored: *storage.*

    - Specify the **Destination node** where this entity should be moved after picking it from the storage cell: *shapePickup.*

    - Select the **Use resources to move** checkbox since we want products to be moved by fork lift trucks.

    - In the **List of resources {pool1, ...}** field, specify the list of names of **NetworkResourcePool** objects defining the resources that should be used to transport products from the storage cells. Type *{forkLiftTrucks}* here.

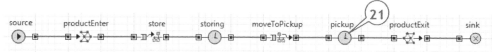

21. This **Delay** object models the time to pick up an entity.

    - Define the object's **Delay time**: *minute().*

    - Select the **Maximum capacity** checkbox.

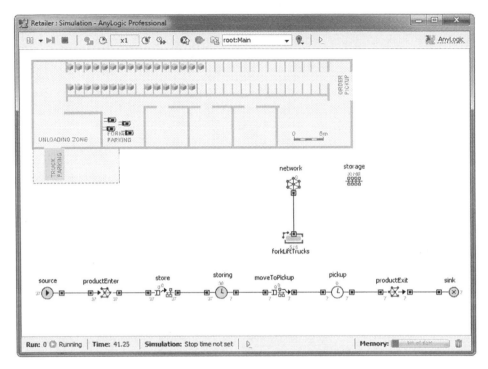

22. Run the model.

When you run the model, you should see how products are delivered to the retailer's unloading zone, placed in the warehouse's storage, and - eventually - taken to the pickup area.

# Phase 2. Adding trucks delivering products

Let's develop our model.

- Assume trucks deliver products to the retailer. Each truck has 10 finished products.

- When a truck arrives, the unloading time is distributed triangularly with parameters: 1, 2, 3 minutes.

- Fork lift trucks take the unloaded products to warehouse cells.

1.  Add a picture of a lorry and then slightly reduce its size.

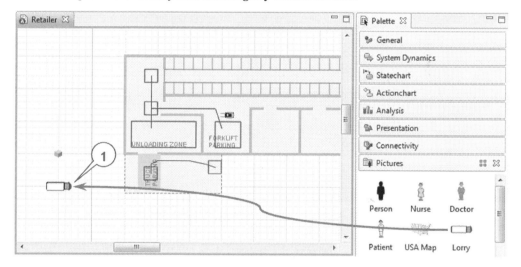

Add new objects into the flowchart to model new logic. Name them as shown in the figure below.

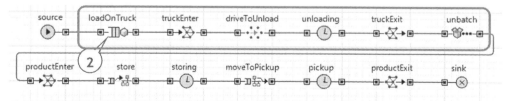

2.  This **Batch** object models creating a batch of products to be delivered to our retailer.

- Clear the **Permanent batch** checkbox to enable unbatching this batch later on individual entities (boxes with washing machines inside).

- Set our *lorry* picture as **Batch animation shape** (the shape that will animate entities-batches, in our case - trucks).

- Select the **Enable rotation** checkbox to enable rotating animations of moving trucks according their headings.

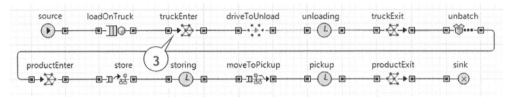

3.   This **NetworkEnter** object adds trucks to our network.

- Specify the network the trucks will enter by typing *network* in the **Network** parameter.

- Define the network node where trucks will appear by specifying *shapeUnloadEntry* as **Entry node**.

- Set the **Speed** of trucks as *2\*meter/second()*.

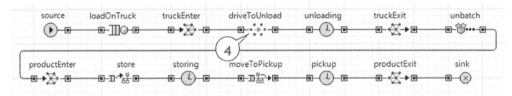

4.   **NetworkMoveTo** object moves the entity to the specified network location. We use it to move trucks from the entry location to the truck unloading zone.

- Specify the destination node in the **Node** field: *shapeTruckUnloading*.

- Type *entity.setOffsets( 0, 0, PI/2);* in the **On exit** field. This way we rotate the animation of the truck as it was back running. *PI* here is mathematical constant π. *PI/2* here specifies the rotation angle equal to 90 degrees.

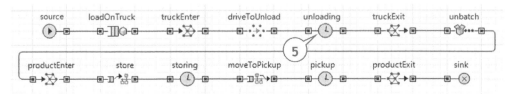

5.  **Delay** object models delay needed to unload boxes from a truck.

    - Define the **Delay time:** *triangular(1, 2, 3)*minute()*

    - Select the **Maximum capacity** checkbox to enable simultaneous unloading of unlimited number of trucks.

*triangular* distribution is often used when there's little or no data to represent the process duration. The function has three parameters: a minimal value, a most likely value, a maximum value.

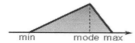

triangular( min, mode, max )

min      mode max

AnyLogic supports more than 30 probability distributions, including uniform, exponential, lognormal, binomial, beta, geometric, and Poisson. You can find a list of the probability distributions in the **AnyLogic Help, AnyLogic Classes and Functions | AnyLogic functions | Probability distributions** section.

*minute* function returns a time value equal to one minute according to the current time unit setting (time units are set up in the model properties).

Let's say seconds are the model's time unit. In this case, minute function returns 60. By multiplying this value, we convert it from minutes to seconds. The same logic works if you choose another time unit, but minute will return another value. Use this way to specify time durations. It makes these values independent from model time unit settings.

6.  This **NetworkExit** object removes trucks that have delivered their cargo from the network.

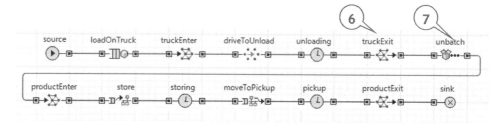

7.  This **Unbatch** object unbatches our batch in original entities and models how boxes are unloaded from a truck.

8.  Run the model. In the **Projects** view, right-click (Mac OS: Ctrl+click) *Simulation* experiment of the model *Retailer* and select **Run** from the popup menu. You should see how trucks deliver products to the warehouse.

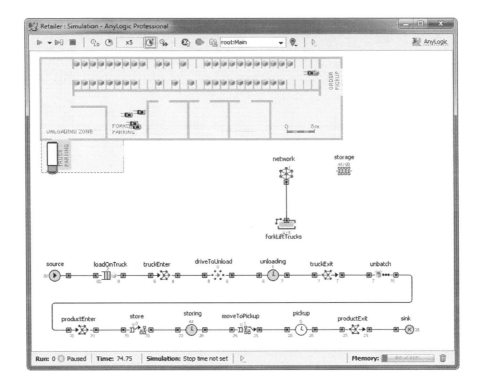

## Experiments

- *Experiment* stores a model's set of configuration parameters. AnyLogic supports several experiment types that address different simulation tasks.

- When a new project is created, one experiment is created automatically: a simulation experiment named *Simulation*.

- *Simulation experiment* runs model simulation with animation displayed and model debugging enabled. Simulation experiment is used in most cases. Other AnyLogic experiments are used when the model parameters play a significant role and you need to analyze how they affect the model behavior, or when you want to find optimal parameter values.

# Phase 3. Implementing inventory replenishment policy

Now we want to apply inventory replenishment policy. We'll implement (s, S) policy:

- There are two inventory levels defined: lower (s) and upper (S).

- Whenever the inventory position (items on hand plus items on order) drops to a given level s or below, an order is placed for a sufficient quantity to bring the inventory position up to a given level S.

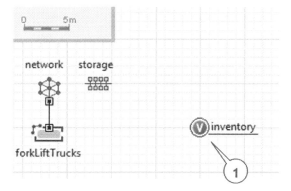

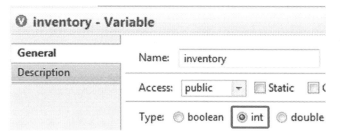

1. Add a variable *inventory* to store the current value of retailer's inventory level. Make this variable integer (*int*) since it will count products.

2. Add a parameter *S* to define the upper inventory level. Make this parameter integer, set its **Default value** equal to a number of cells in the retailer's warehouse (*60*) and type *applyInventoryPolicy()*; in its **On change** code. This code will recalculate the retailer's inventory policy by calling the function we'll define later on.

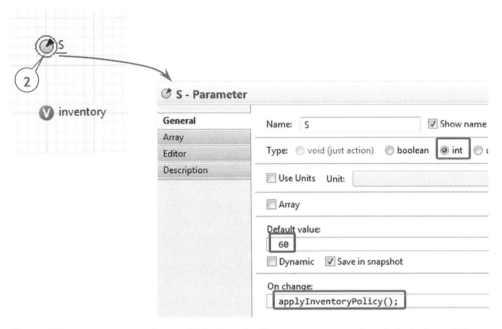

3. Add a parameter *s* that will define the lower inventory level. Ctrl+drag (Mac OS: Cmd+drag) *S* parameter to create its copy. Rename it to *s* and set its **Default value** equal to *10*.

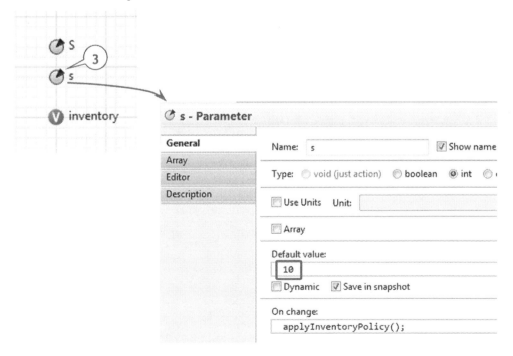

Here we can see that similar things are defined with different elements – *variable* and *parameter*.

## Parameters vs. variables: what to use?

- Parameters typically define the modeled object's static characteristics. A parameter is normally a constant in a single simulation, and you change it only when you need to adjust your model's behavior.

- Variables typically store a model simulation's results or they model data units that change over time.

Now, we'll define an algorithm to check the inventory level and - if it is low - order new products. Let's use an action chart to graphically define this algorithm.

## Action charts

- An *action chart* is a structured block chart that allows you to graphically define an algorithm. It is made from blocks on the **Actionchart** palette.

- Action charts are very helpful - they allow you to define algorithms even if you aren't familiar with Java operator syntax.

- Action charts give you one more obvious benefit: they visualize the implemented algorithms and make them more intuitive to other users.

4. Start drawing an action chart with adding the **Action Chart** element. Drag the **Action Chart** element from the **Actionchart** palette. **Action Chart** creates the basic action chart consisting of a starting point and "return" block. From this point on, you must insert required action chart blocks into their places inside the created action chart according to the algorithm's logic.

5. Name the action chart *applyInventoryPolicy*.

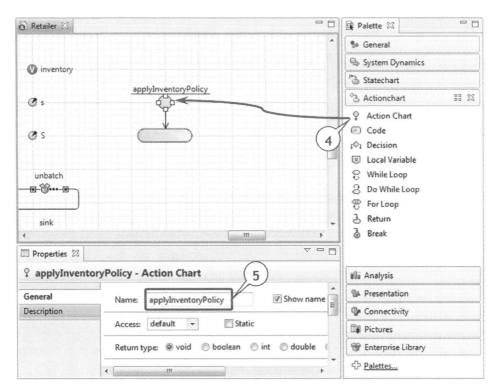

6. Drag the **Decision** element from the **Actionchart** palette on to the action chart's branch. We want our algorithm to check a condition and then use the result to perform an action. The best way to implement this is to use a **Decision** block.

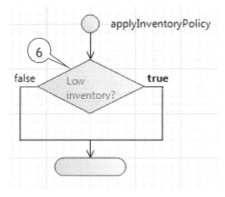

**Decision** block is the simplest way to route the algorithm flow. The block has two exit branches - *true* and *false*. You can define an action sequence for either branch using other action chart blocks. When the control reaches the "decision" block, if the specified condition evaluates to *true*, *true* branch is taken. Otherwise, *false* branch is taken.

7.  Modify the decision block's properties. Define the **Condition:** *inventory < s.* Here we determine if current inventory level is lower than the defined lower level s. Specify **Comments:** *Low inventory?* (they will be visible in the graphical diagram).

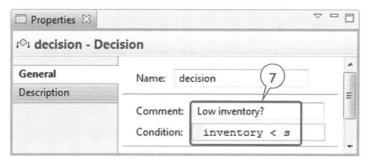

## Adding blocks into an action chart

As you drag an action chart block from the palette and move the mouse over your action chart, you'll see insertion points on the action chart branches indicated with little green circles. To add a block into a branch, release the mouse button after you place it on top of the required insertion point.

Place two blocks in the *true* branch of the **Decision** block to implement ordering products if the inventory level is low.

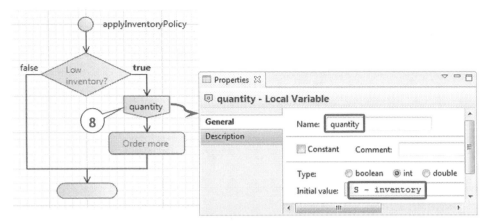

8.   First, add **Local variable** from the **Actionchart** palette. **Local variable** block is used to define a variable inside an action chart. Such variable is visible only down the action chart starting from the declaration point. Local variable *quantity* will calculate the quantity of products that should be ordered by evaluating the gap between the upper level *S* and the current inventory level: *S - inventory*

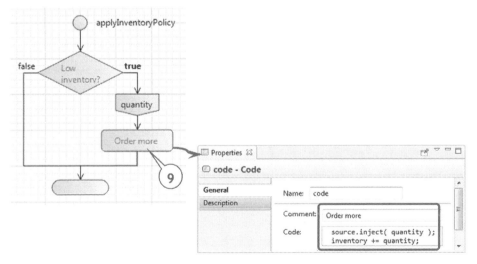

9.   Then add **Code** block. This block will execute the following code (define it in the **Code** property):

*source.inject(quantity);*

*inventory += quantity;*

**Code** block allows you to insert a code snippet that performs an action into your action chart. Code can be a single Java statement or a set of statements terminated by a semicolon.

The first line prompts the *source* object to generate a number of entities (equal to *quantity*), and the second line increases the inventory level by this value.

Optionally you can add *Order more* comment for the block to explain its meaning to others. The comments will be shown inside the block instead of the code.

Let's look at the action chart to better understand its role. **Decision** block assesses our inventory level (*inventory < s*). If we need more products, it creates the *quantity* variable and assigns the number of required goods (*s - inventory*) to it. Then we create this number of products by calling *source.inject(quantity);*. Finally, we recalculate the *inventory* level.

We want to check inventory level at model startup and on every new product shipment. First, we'll implement checking at startup.

10. Select *Main* in the project tree.

11. To execute the algorithm at model startup, we place the call of the actionchart in the **Startup code** of our *Main* class. Type *applyInventoryPolicy();* here.

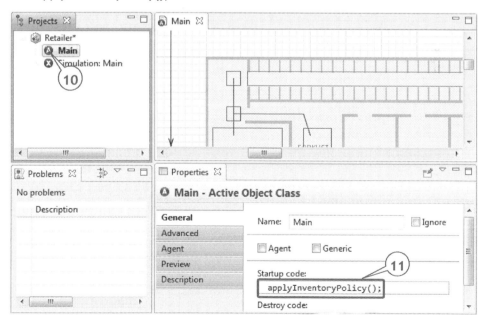

Startup code is executed at the model initialization's final stage after the model's objects are constructed, connected, and initialized, and before anything else is done. This is a place for additional initialization and starting object's activities such as events.

## How to execute an algorithm defined with an action chart?

- Action charts are executed the same way as functions - you call an action chart followed by parentheses in the code:

  *applyInventoryPolicy();*

- If an action chart has arguments, you should pass the argument values - separated by commas – by placing them in parentheses. For example:

  *moveTo(15, 20);*

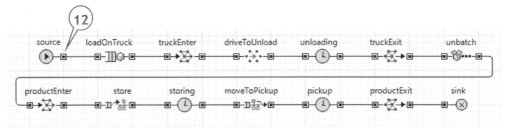

12. Change entity generation mode of *source* object. Choose **Manual (call inject())** option in the **Arrivals defined by** parameter. Let it generate entities not with the specified rate but on *inject()* method calls (you should remember we've placed such a call into the *code* block of *applyInventoryPolicy* actionchart).

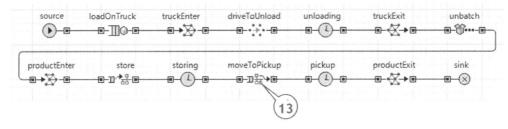

13. Define actions to be executed on shipping the product from the warehouse. Type the following code in the **On exit** parameter of the *moveToPickup* block:

    *inventory--;*
    *applyInventoryPolicy();*

This code implements inventory check on every new shipment to a customer. The first line decrements the current inventory level by one item, and the second line executes the actionchart to determine if the factory needs to order new products.

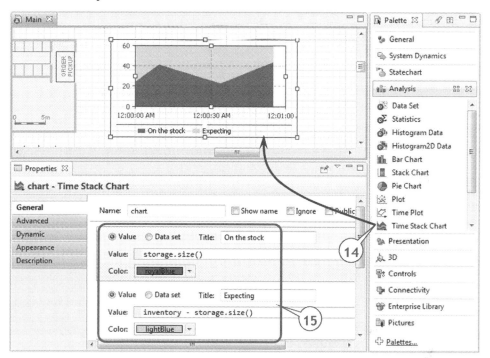

Add a chart to display the number of products stored in the warehouse and the number of products expected to be delivered to the retailer.

14. The best way to visualize the inventory dynamics is to use time stack chart. Add **Time stack chart** from the **Analysis** palette and then resize it as shown above.

15. Add two data items, one to display **Value** *storage.size()* with **Title** *On the stock* and the other to display *inventory - storage.size()* with **Title** *Expecting*.

16. Modify the chart properties:

- In the **Time Window** box, change the chart's time window to one week.

- In the **Vertical scale** box, click **Fixed** scale with a maximum Y-axis value of *60*.

- In the **Recurrence time** box, type *hour()* to update recurrence time to one hour.

- In the **Display up to** box, change the number of samples the chart displays at one time to *200*.

17. In the **Time axis format** list, click **Model date (date only)**.

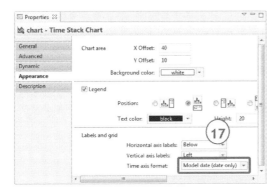

Charts with history (time plot, time stack chart and time color chart) can display model dates in time (x-) axis labels. Select the suggested format that best fits your needs in the **Time axis format** option on the **Appearance** properties page.

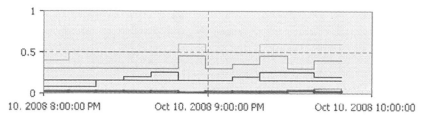

Add two sliders to vary *s* and *S* parameters interactively during the simulation.

**18.** Add **Slider** from the **Controls** palette on to the diagram.

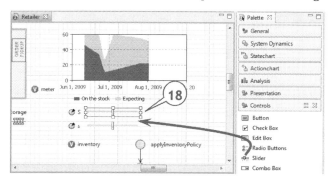

**19.** Modify the slider's properties by selecting the **Link to** checkbox and then typing the name of parameter you want to vary in the edit box to the right: *S*. Set the **Maximum value** equal to *60*.

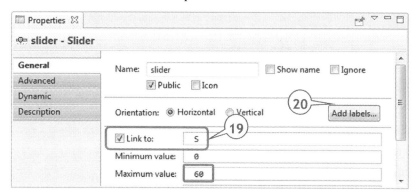

**20.** Add labels that display the slider's minimum, current, and maximum values by clicking **Add labels**.

**21.** Create a copy of this slider and set it up to vary *s* parameter. Use Ctrl+drag (Mac OS: Cmd+drag) to copy.

**22.** Add labels for this slider also.

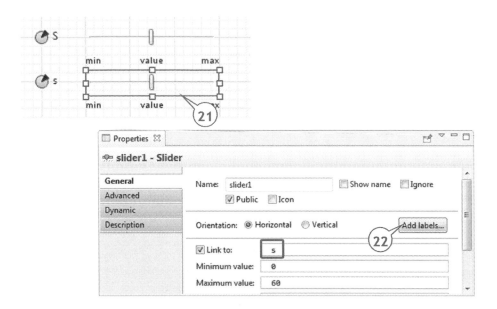

Expand the presentation window to fit the new elements.

23. In the project tree, select the experiment item *Simulation: Main* to show its properties.

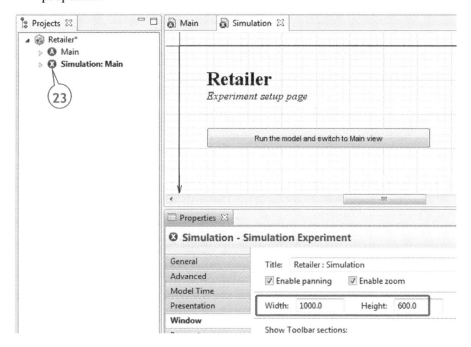

24. Go to the **Window** properties page, set the frame's width to *1000* while leaving the default height at *600*. This is how you specify the presentation window's initial size.

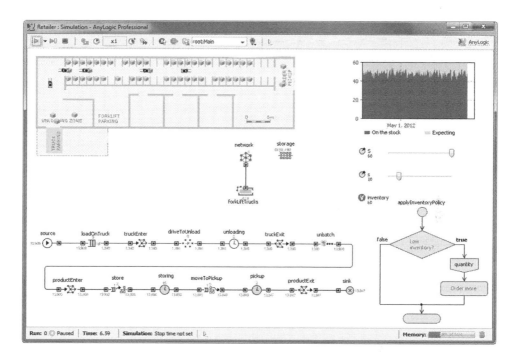

25. Run the model and play with the sliders. You can see how the model behavior depends on the inventory replenishment policy.

# Phase 4. Adding 3D animation

Create a 3D animation of the retailer that will work in parallel with 2D animation.

1.  Open the **3D** palette and drag the **3D Window** object below the flowchart.

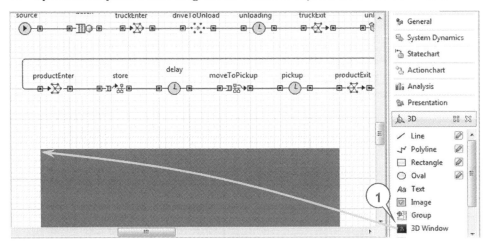

## *3D Window*

- AnyLogic shows the 3D animation in 3D windows. There can be multiple 3D windows showing the 3D scene from different perspectives.

- 3D animation windows will work in parallel and with 2D animation.

2.  Right-click (Mac OS: Ctrl+click) the canvas, and choose **Unlock all shapes** from the context menu.

3.  Select the background image, and then check **Show in 3D scene** in its properties.

4.  Select the **Lock** checkbox to lock this image.

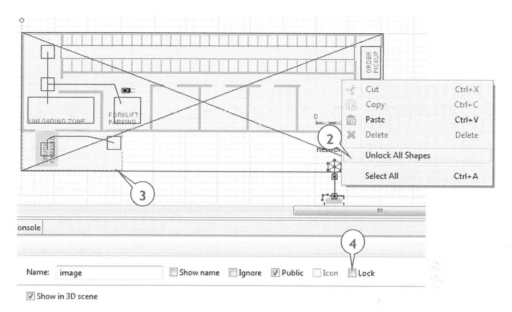

The first object we'll show in 3D is the floor plan. By default, most shapes will not show in 3D unless you select the **Show in 3D scene** checkbox.

5.  Run the model. Select the **[window3d]** view area on the toolbar.

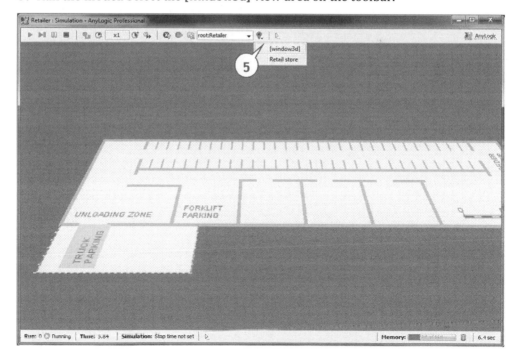

## Default view area for 3D window

- When you create a 3D window, AnyLogic adds a view area that allows you to easily navigate to the 3D view at runtime. The view area expands the 3D window to the model window's full size.

- To choose the view area, click the toolbar's **Navigate to view area** button.

6. Delete the 2D picture of the forklift truck.

7. Drag the **Fork Lift Truck** object from the **3D objects** palette to the same place. We are simply substituting the 2D picture with 3D object for forklift truck.

8. Change the object's name to *fork*. Name the 3D object shape *fork* since we used this name for fork animation shape.

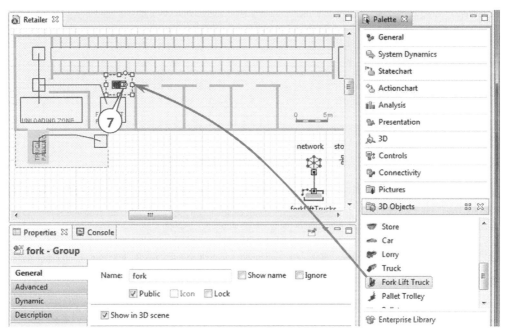

## 3D Objects palette

- The **3D Objects** palette contains frequently used 3D objects. If the palette doesn't have the object you want, you can import an object from a .x3d file.

- When a 3D object is added to the model, AnyLogic also creates its 2D representation, which is shown in the graphical editor and in 2D animation at runtime.

**9.** Select the network group and check **Show in 3D** scene in its properties.

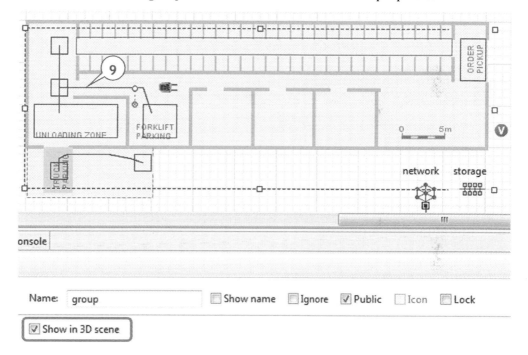

**10.** Right-click (Mac OS: Ctrl+click) any network shape, and choose **Select Group Contents** from the popup menu.

**11.** On the **Advanced** page of the group contents properties set the **Z-Height** to 0.

Unless you mark the network group as "3D," the network's moving objects will not appear in the 3D scene.

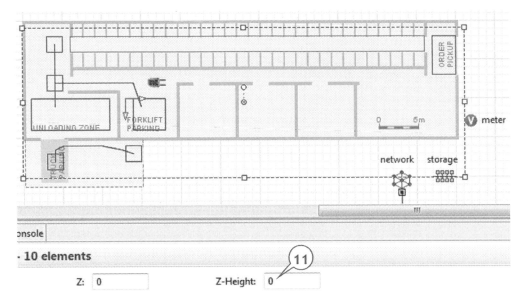

**· 10 elements**

Z:  0                    Z-Height:  0    11

We don't need the network shapes to have Z-Height, so we are resetting that property.

## Z-Height property

- When you select a shape's **Show in 3D scene** property, AnyLogic automatically sets the shape's height to 10 so that it has "volume" in 3D.

- If you set the same property for a group of shapes, it will apply to all of the group's shapes.

12. Run the model.

Display the 3D window, and watch the forklift trucks as they move through the warehouse. If you want a different perspective, you can use your mouse to navigate within the 3D scene.

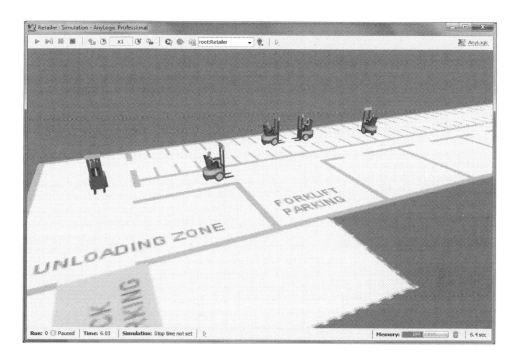

## Navigation in 3D scene

- **Drag the mouse** to move the camera right, left, forward, or backward at the same height.

- **Rotate the mouse wheel** to move the camera closer or further from the scene's center.

- **Press and hold Alt as you drag the mouse** to rotate the scene relative to the camera.

Like the forklift truck, we're replacing the box's 2D picture with the 3D picture.

13. Delete the box's 2D picture (packaged product).

14. Since the **3D objects** palette doesn't have a box, we can use the 3D rectangle to create our own (that is, the rectangle with Z-height). Drag the **Rectangle** object from the **3D** palette in the same place.

15. Set the 3D rectangle's size to 10x10 pixels.

16. Change the 3D rectangle's name to *pictureBox.*

17. Set the 3D rectangle's **Fill color** to **Textures.. | floorWood** and **Line color** to **No line.**

If a shape with Z-height doesn't have line color, its vertical sides use the fill color.

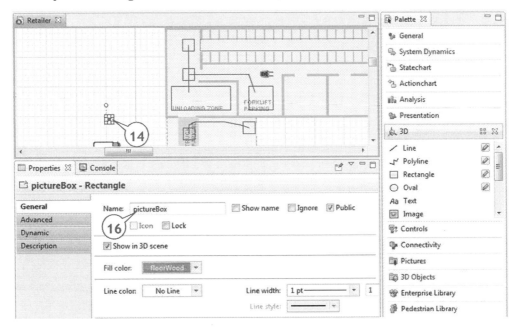

## The "3D versions" of line, polyline, rectangle, and oval

- You can find these four shapes in the **Presentation** and **3D** palettes. By default, the **3D** palette's shapes have the **Show in 3D scene** property selected and **Z-Height** set to 10.

18. Delete the lorry's 2D picture.

19. Drag the **Lorry** object from the **3D Objects** palette.

Again, we're substituting the 2D shape with the 3D shape. Since the 3D **Lorry** object's default name is also *lorry*, we don't need to change the name.

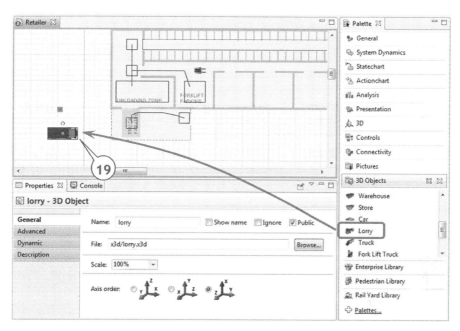

Complete the final decoration of the warehouse.

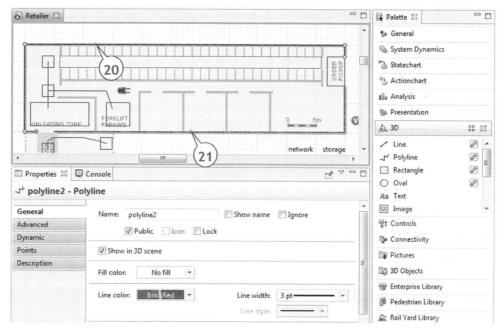

**20.** In the **3D** palette, double-click the **Polyline** object, and then draw a polyline over the warehouse's outside wall from Unloading zone to Order pickup.

21. Draw a second polyline over the remaining part of the wall.

22. Select both polylines and set:

   - On the **General** page:

   - **Line color:  Textures.. | brickRed**

   - **Line width:** *3pt*

   - On the **Advanced** page:

   - **Z-Height:** *30*

23. Run the model.

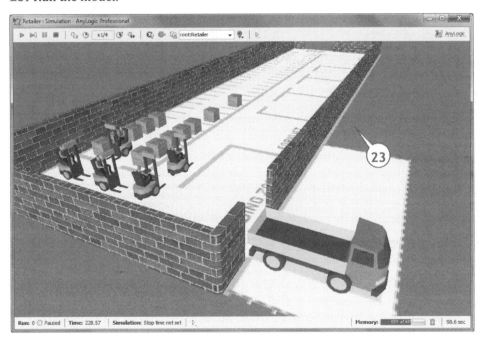

We've completed the warehouse model. Though our model represents a small warehouse, you'll be pleased to know the model's complexity isn't directly related to the warehouse's size. In fact, it is largely a function of the detail level you select and the complexity of the related business processes.

To make this model more realistic, you can add dispatch process, picking process, additional zones: unloading zone, reception zone, placement zone, dispatch zone, control zone, temporary storage area,  more types of staff: acceptors, controllers, different type of vehicles etc.

# Agent-based modeling[2]

*Agent based modeling* is much newer than system dynamics or discrete event modeling. In fact, agent based modeling was largely an academic topic until simulation practitioners began using it in 2002-2003.

It was triggered by:

- Desire to gain deeper insights into the systems traditional modeling approaches don't capture well

- Advances in modeling technology from computer science, including object oriented modeling, UML, and statecharts

- The rapid growth of CPU power and memory. Agent based models are more demanding than system dynamics and discrete event models.

Agent based modeling offers a modeler yet another way to look at the system:

🌢 **You may not know how the system behaves, what its key variables and their dependencies might be, or even see a process flow, but you may have some insight into how the system's objects behave individually. If that's the case, you can start building the model by identifying the objects (agents) and defining their behaviors. Sometimes you would connect the agents and let them interact, sometimes you would put them in an environment, which may have its own dynamics. The global behavior of the system then emerges out of many (tens, hundreds, thousands, millions) concurrent individual behaviors.**

There's no standard language for agent based modeling, and an agent based model's structure comes from graphical editors or scripts. Agent behavior is specified in many ways. Frequently agent has a notion of state and its actions and reactions depend on the state; then behavior is best defined with statecharts. Sometimes behavior is defined in rules executed upon special events.

In many cases, you can best capture the agent's internal dynamics using system dynamics or a discrete event approach, and then put a stock and flow diagram or

---

[2] The introduction is from "The Book of AnyLogic" (working title) being currently written by Dr. Andrei Borshchev.

a process flowchart inside an agent. Similarly, outside agents the dynamics of the environment where they live is often naturally modeled using traditional methods. It's why a good number of agent based models are multi-method models.

Academics still debate which properties an object should have to be called an "agent": proactive and reactive qualities, a spatial awareness, an ability to learn, social ability, "intellect", etc. In applied agent based modeling, however, you'll find all kinds of agents: some communicate while others live in total isolation, some live in a space while others live without a space, some learn and adapt while others never change their behavior patterns.

Here are some useful facts to ensure you aren't misguided by academic literature and various theories of agent based modeling:

- **Agents are not the same thing as cellular automata** and they don't have to live in discrete space (like the grid in The Game of Life). In many agent based models space is not present. When space is needed, in most cases it is continuous, sometimes a geographical map or a facility floor plan.

- **Agents are not necessarily people.** Anything can be an agent: a vehicle, a piece of equipment, a project, an idea, an organization, or even an investment. A model of a steel converter plant where each machine is modeled as an active object and their interactions produce steel is an agent based model.

- **An object that seems to be absolutely passive can be an agent.** For example, you can model a water supply network's pipe segment as an agent: we can associate maintenance and replacement schedules, costs, and breakdown events with it.

- **There can be many and can be very few agents in an agent based model**. Agents can be of the same type and can be different types.

- **There are agent based models where agents don't interact.** The health economics field, as an example, uses alcohol use, obesity, and chronic disease models where individual dynamics depends only on personal parameters and, sometimes, on the environment.

## Market Model

We'll build a model of a consumer market to better understand how a new product enters the market. We'll model it in agent based way where each consumer will be an agent. Market simulation is typical application of agent-based modeling since there is always some stochastics in human decisions.

Let's assume the following are true:

- There are 5000 people who don't use the product, but advertizing and word of mouth will eventually lead them to purchase it

- If a person wants to buy the product, but it is not available for some time, he decides not to buy it and becomes a potential user again.

- Any product discards in the specified discard time and generates the immediate need to buy a replacement.

# Phase 1. Considering the influence of advertizing

We'll start with a simple case that leaves aside product discards or agent-to-agent communication. For now, we'll model how consumers purchase the product because of advertizing.

Initially consumers are not using the product, but are all potentially interested (are potential users).

Advertizing generates the demand for the product, and the percentage of potential users that become ready to buy the product during a given day is determined by *Advertizing effectiveness = 0.1*.

1. Open the model creation wizard by choosing **File|New|Model** from the main menu.

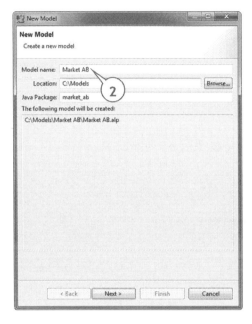

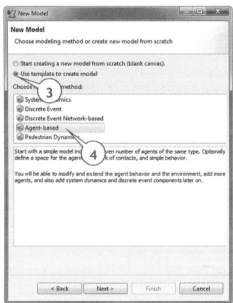

2. In the **Model name** box, name the model *Market AB* (AB is an abbrevation for Agent Based) and then click **Next**.

3. We'll use the AnyLogic model creation wizard to create our model - it's the best option for creating agent based models. Doing this we enable choosing a model template for our model's base Select the **Use template to create a model** option.

4. AnyLogic provides a comprehensive set of model templates, and each template works with a specific modeling approach. In the **Choose modeling method** list, click the **Agent-based** option, and then click **Next**.

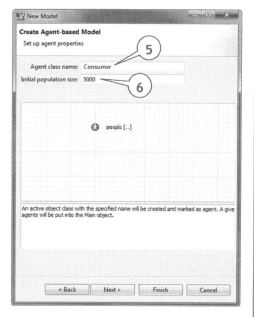

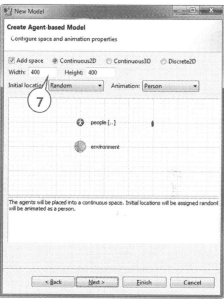

5. Each agent will be modeled as an instance of special active object class declared as an agent. You can set the name of this class in the wizard. Type *Consumer* in the **Agent class name** edit box.

6. Define the number of agents in the model by typing *5000* in the **Initial population size** box. AnyLogic will create 5000 instances of *Consumer* class, and each instance models a specific agent-consumer. Click **Next**.

7. Our agents will live in one environment. In AnyLogic, environment is a special construct that defines the shared properties of a group of agents. While you don't have to define the environment in your agent based model, the environment makes some agent-specific functionality available.

   In this case, we define continuous environment and set the environment's **Width** and **Height** to 400. The agents will be visualized in a 400x400 pixel rectangle. Click **Next**.

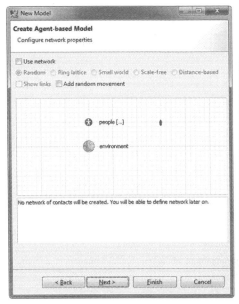

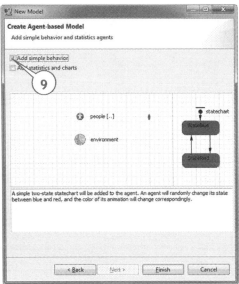

Finish configuring the model on the last two wizard pages.

8. The wizard's next page allows you to define our agent population's connection network. Since we don't want to create an agent network, click **Next** to go to the wizard's final page.

9. Select the **Add simple behavior** checkbox to tell AnyLogic we want our agents to have the simplest behavior defined by a statechart, and then click **Finish**.

When finished, you can see the agent based model we've created. Our model has two active object classes: *Main* and *Consumer*.

- *Consumer* class is declared as agent class (this enables some useful AnyLogic services for agents, for example communication, space, layout, etc.) The class has agent's picture and a statechart defining its behavior.

- *Main* class has replicated object *people* 🧍 (containing a set of objects of class *Consumer*) modeling agents and **Environment** 🌐 inside. Environment takes care of the agents' space, layout, network, and communication. In our case, we need an environment to lay out the agent presentations and later to model word of mouth by agent-to-agent interaction.

## Active objects

- Active objects are a model's main building blocks, and you can use them to model real-world objects such as processing stations, resources, people, physical objects, controllers, and trucks.

- Each active object typically represents one of the model's logical sections. This enables you to decompose a model into many levels of detail as required.

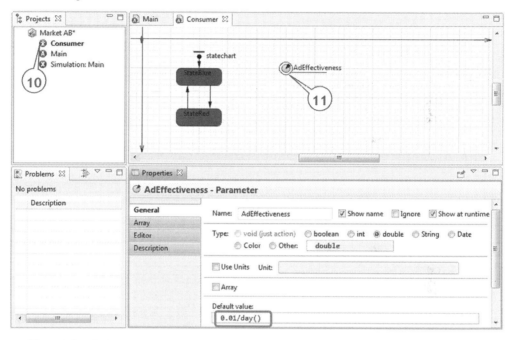

We'll start by defining consumer characteristics and behavior.

10. Open the *Consumer* diagram by double-clicking it in the **Projects** view. You'll see the class' graphical diagram and the two-state statechart created by the model creation wizard.

11. Add the *AdEffectiveness* parameter.

   The parameter will define the percentage of potential users that become ready to buy the product due because of advertising during a day. We assume an average of 1% of potential users want to buy the product during a day, so we specify *0.01/day()* as the parameter's **Default value**.

We'll define a consumer's behavior as a two state sequence:

- *PotentialUser* - consumers in this state are only potentially interested in buying the product.

- *User* – consumer in this state have purchased the product.

Modify the statechart automatically created by the model creation wizard:

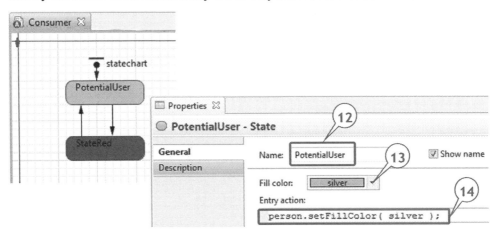

12. Name the upper state *PotentialUser*.

13. Change the state's color to *silver* using the **Fill color** list.

14. Substitute the state's **Entry action** with *person.setFillColor(silver);*

    This way we'll change the consumer presentation's color to silver to visualize its state change. Here, *person* is the name of consumer's presentation shape the model creation wizard created.

15. Modify the lower state's properties in the same way:

    **Name:** *User*

    **Entry action:** *person.setFillColor(limeGreen);*

16. Change the state's color.

    To choose a specific color, choose **Other colors** from the **Fill color** list, and then use the **Colors** dialog box to select the color (*limeGreen*).

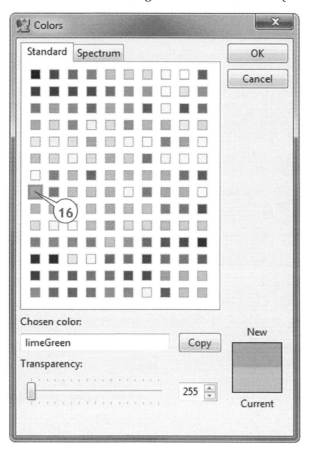

17. The transition from *PotentialUser* to *User* state will model how a person buys the product because of its advertising. Name this transition *Ad*, and let the rate *AdEffectiveness* trigger it.

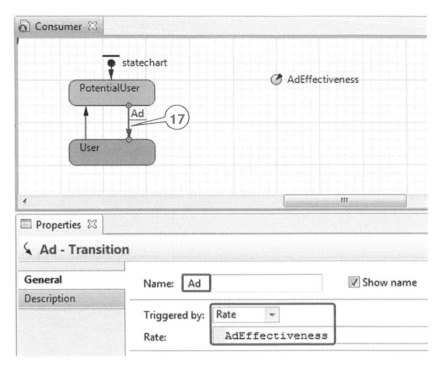

Transition of rate type is the same as transition triggered by a stochastic timeout distributed exponentially. When the statechart enters the state *PotentialUser*, a draw from the exponential distribution is made and the timeout is set up. As a result, each consumer's adoption time will differ because of advertizing, though an average 1% of potential users will buy the product in one day.

18. Delete the transition from the lower to the upper state since at this phase we assume the consumer doesn't change his decision to buy the product.

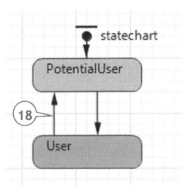

19. Open *Main* diagram, and then rename the replicated object *people* to *consumers*.

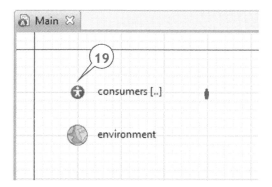

20. Run the model. Speed up the simulation to *10x*. You should see the population gradually turn green - the effect of advertizing - until every consumer buys the product.

When an agent purchases the product because of advertizing, its state *User* becomes active and the state's **Entry action** is executed. As you may remember, this action changes the agent animation shape's color to *limeGreen*, and that's why agent animations gradually turn green as more people purchase the product.

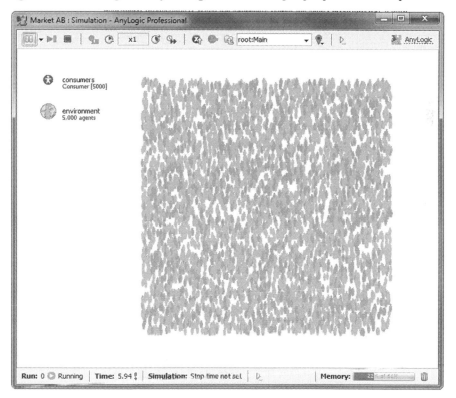

# Phase 2. Adding a chart to visualize the model output

We want to know how many people have purchased our product at a given moment. With that in mind, we'll define functions to count our product's users and potential users, and then add a chart to show the dynamics.

1.  First, define a function to count potential users. To add a new function collecting statistics over agents, open the diagram of the active object class *Main*, select the object *consumers*, and go to its **Statistics** properties page.

2.  Click the **Add statistics** button.

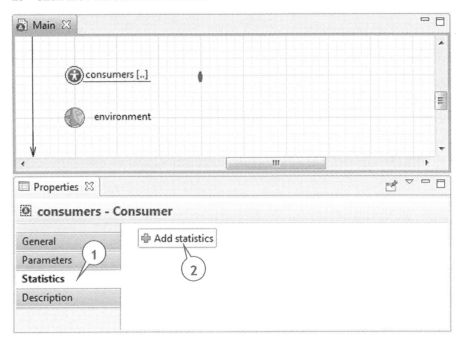

We need to iterate through the agents to find out how many are in the state *PotentialUser*.

3.  Define the function of type **Count** with **Name** *NPotential*. The statistics of type **count** iterates through a population and counts how many agents satisfy the given condition.

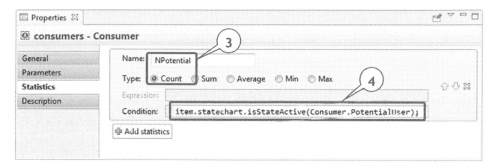

4.  Enter *item.statechart.isStateActive(Consumer.PotentialUser);* as the function **Condition**.

    *item* represents the agent being checked in the iteration loop, *statechart* is the consumer's statechart name, *isStateActive()* is a standard statechart method that checks whether the specified state is active, and *PotentialUser* is the name of the state defined in the agent - and that is why it needs the classname prefix *Consumer*.

5.  Define one more statistics function to calculate the number of product users. Name it *NUser* and let it count the number of agents, conforming the **Condition** *item.statechart.isStateActive(Consumer.User);* You can simply copy the condition from the item *NPotential* and modify it slightly.

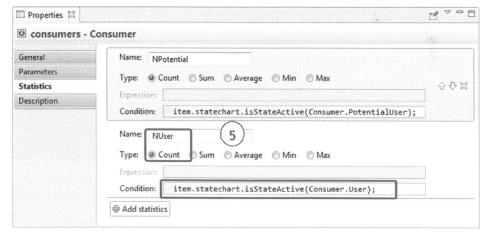

6.  On *Main* diagram, move the consumer's picture (the presentation of the embedded consumer) to the position (300,200).

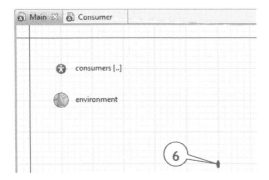

7.  Drag the **Time Stack Chart** from the **Analysis** palette on to the *Main* diagram. With this chart, we'll visualize the dynamics of users and potential users over time.

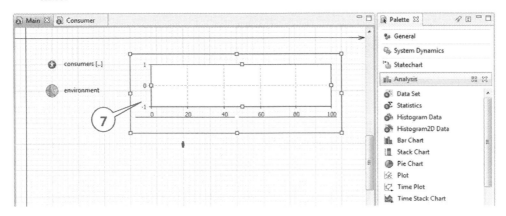

## How to know what class is edited currently?

- You have two active object classes in your model. Now you occasionally open a diagram of this or that class and finally a question may come up: what class am I editing in the graphical editor?

- To make things clear, AnyLogic selects the tab of the currently opened class in the graphical editor and also emphasizes its item in the **Projects** tree:

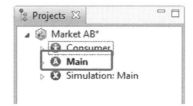

8.  Add two data items for the chart to display:

- *consumers.NUser()* with title *Users* and color *limeGreen* (you may find this color in the section above the **Other Colors...** section of the popup **Color** window)

- *consumers.NPotential()* with title *Potential users* and color *silver.*

Here we call our statistics functions *NUser* and *NPotential* we've defined for *consumers* object on the previous step.

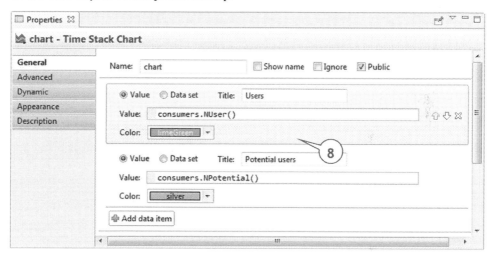

9.  Set **Time Window** as *365 * day()*
    Set the **Vertical scale** of the chart as **Fixed** to *5000*
    Specify the recurrence time of chart's update: *day()*
    Set **Display up to** *365* latest samples.

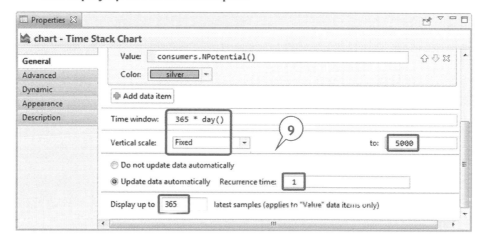

10. Go to the time stack chart's **Appearance** properties, and then set it to display model date (and only dates) near the time axis.

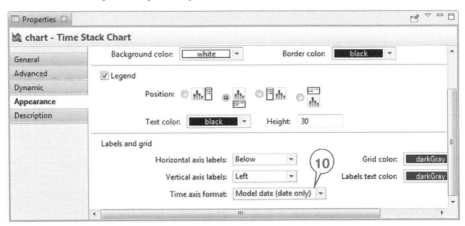

11. Open the model properties by clicking the **Projects** tree's top object (*Market AB*).

12. Choose *days* as model **Time units**.

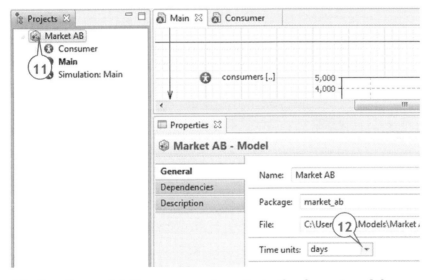

13. Run the model. Now you can investigate the dynamics of the process using our time stack color chart.

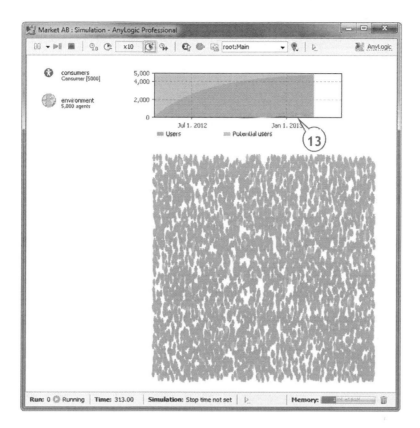

# Phase 3. Adding word of mouth effect

In this phase, we'll model how people persuade others to purchase our product. For simplicity, we'll call this the word of mouth effect.

- Let consumers contact each other. On average, a consumer contacts one person a day.

- During these consumer meetings, our product's current users may influence potential users. We'll define the probability of the potential user buying the product as *AdoptionFraction=0.01*.

1. Open the *Consumer* diagram, and then add a *ContactRate* parameter. We'll use it to define a consumer's average daily contacts. Set **Default value:** *1/day()*

2. Add an *AdoptionFraction* parameter.

   This parameter will define a person's influence on others, a number we'll express as the percentage of people who will use the product after they come into contact with the consumer. Set **Default value:** *0.01*

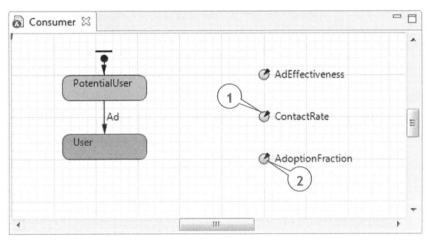

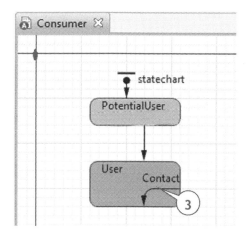

3.  Draw a transition inside the *User* state. Since internal and external transitions behave differently, the transition should lie completely ***inside*** the state.

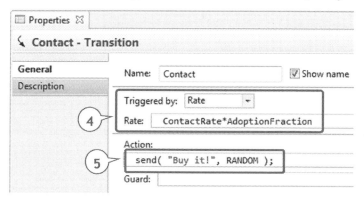

4.  Modify the transition properties. This transition will occur with the specified **Rate** *ContactRate\*AdoptionFraction*

5.  Specify the **Action** that will be executed on triggering this transition: *send( "Buy it!", RANDOM );*

Since we want our product's users to talk to potential users, we'll set up a cyclic transition in the state *User*. Each time the transition occurs, the agent-user will send a message to another random agent about our product. If the agent who receives the message is a potential user (in other words, the receiving agent is in the state *PotentialUser*), his state will change to *User*. We'll do this by adding a transition from *PotentialUser* to *User* that will be triggered by this message.

In the transition action, the consumer chooses another random consumer – not necessarily the potential user – and sends him a *"Buy it!"* text message. This is done with the code *send( "Buy it!", RANDOM );*

In a perfect world, every contact would lead to a sale, and our rate value would be *ContactRate*. However, we know many of our contacts will not convince potential users to buy our product, and we'll model only a "successful fraction" of contacts by multiplying by *AdoptionFraction=0.01*.

## Internal transitions

- An internal transition is a cyclic transition that lies inside a state, and the transition's start and end points lie on the state's border

- Since an internal transition doesn't exit the enclosing state, it doesn't take the statechart out of this state. Neither the exit nor entry actions are executed when the transition occurs, and the current simple state in the state is not exited.

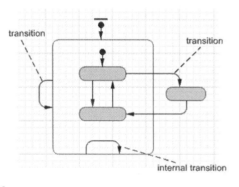

We've set up the agents-users to periodically contact other agents by sending them the message *"Buy it!"*. Let's add a transition to react to this signal.

6.  Draw another transition from *PotentialUser* to *User* state, and then name it *WOM*. This transition will model purchases caused by word of mouth.

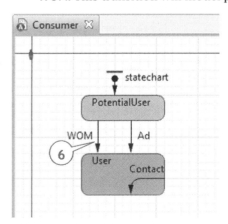

7. On the **General** tab of the **Properties** view, do the following:

   - In the **Triggered by** list, click **Message**.

   - In the **Message** type area, select **String**.

   - In the **Fire transition** area, select **If message equals**, and then type *"Buy it!"*

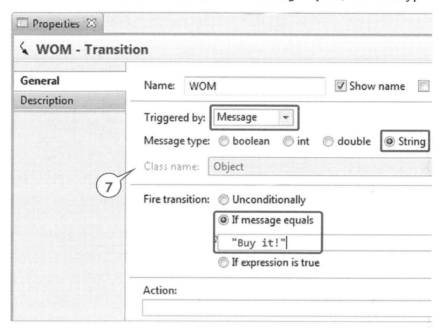

This is the last step in modeling word of mouth. AnyLogic forwards the message from another agent to the statechart, and, if the statechart is in the state *PotentialUser*, it causes an immediate transition to the *User* state. In any other state, the message is ignored.

8. Run the model.

You should see the market saturation occur more quickly now. The chart shows the well-known S-shaped product adoption curve.

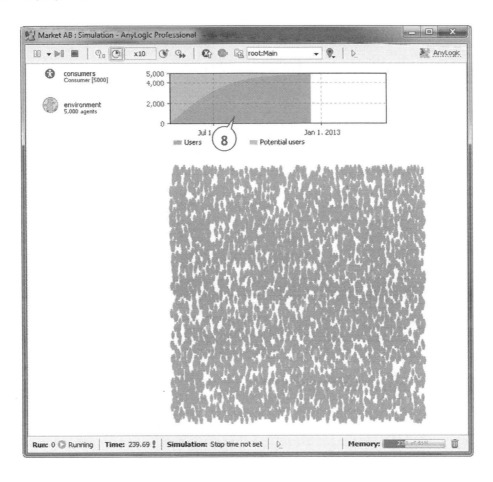

# Phase 4. Considering product discards

In this phase, we'll model product discards.

- Let's assume the average duration of our products' active use is one year.

- Since users eventually discard the product, they'll need to buy replacements. We'll model repeat purchase behavior by assuming adopters become potential adopters when they discard or consume their first units (in other words, the *User* changes state back to the *PotentialUser*).

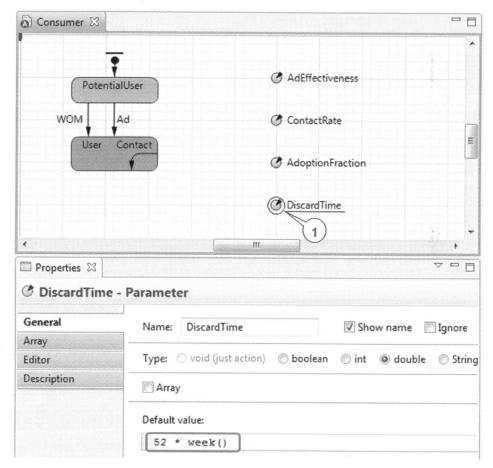

1. Open the *Consumer* diagram, and then add *DiscardTime* parameter.

This parameter will define our product's lifespan: *52\*week()*. We assume users stop using the product after one year.

2. Draw a transition from *User* to *PotentialUser* state, and then name it *Discard*. This transition will model product discards.

3. Set the transition to be triggered by a constant timeout *DiscardTime*.

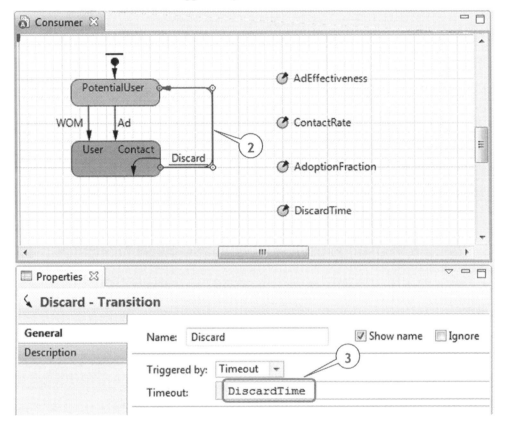

Note the transition *Contact* will not reset that timeout as it is an internal transition.

This is the final step in modeling the product discards, and any product discards in the specified discard time generate an immediate need to buy a replacement.

4. Run the model and watch how discards affect adoption dynamics.

Even after our product saturates the market – where everyone is using our product – you'll notice product discards cause occasional disruptions.

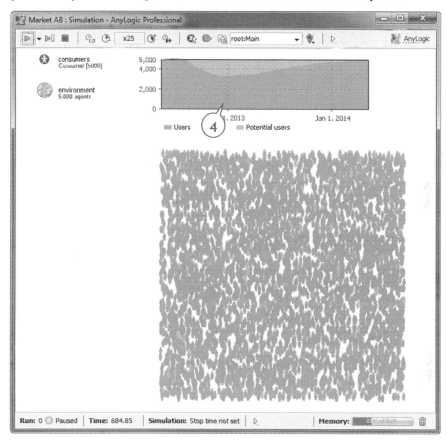

# System Dynamics modeling

*"System dynamics is a perspective and set of conceptual tools that enable us to understand the structure and dynamics of complex systems. System dynamics is also a rigorous modeling method that enables us to build formal computer simulations of complex systems and use them to design more effective policies and organizations."*

*John Sterman, "Business Dynamics:*
*Systems Thinking and Modeling for a Complex World"*

The *system dynamics* method was created in 1950s by MIT Professor Jay Forrester. Drawing on his science and engineering background, Forrester sought to use the laws of physics, in particular the laws of electrical circuits, to describe and investigate the dynamics of economic and social systems. The range of System Dynamics applications includes also urban and ecological systems.

System Dynamics is mostly used in long-term, strategic models, and it assumes high levels of object aggregation: SD models represent people, products, events, and other discrete items by their quantities.

System dynamics is a methodology to study dynamic systems. It suggests you:

- Model the system as a causally closed structure that defines its own behavior.

- Discover the system's feedback loops (circular causality) balancing or reinforcing. Feedback loops are the heart of system dynamics.

- Identify stocks (accumulations) and flows that affect them.

Stocks are accumulations and characterize the system state. They are the memory of the system and sources of disequilibrium. The model works only with aggregates - the stock's items are indistinguishable. Flows are the rates at which these system states change.

If you're having difficulty distinguishing stocks and flows, consider how we measure them.  Stocks are usually expressed in quantities such as people, inventory levels, money, or knowledge - while flows are typically measurements of quantities per time period such as clients per month or dollars per year.

This chapter's purpose is to teach you to develop system dynamics models in AnyLogic rather than teaching you the system dynamics approach. If you want more information about the approach, we recommend you read "<u>Business Dynamics: Systems Thinking and Modeling for a Complex World</u>" by John Sterman.

# SEIR Model

We'll build a model to display the spread of a contagious disease among a large population.

- Consider a population of *TotalPopulation* = 10,000 people. At first, only one person is infectious, and everyone else is susceptible.

- During the infectious phase, an average person comes in contact with *ContactRateInfectious* = 1.25 people each day.

- If an infectious person comes into contact with a susceptible person, the latter person's probability of infection is *Infectifity* = 0.6.

- After a person is infected, a latent phase lasts for *AverageIncubationTime* = 10 days. We'll term people in the latent phase exposed.

- The average illness duration after the latent phase (in other words, the infectious phase's duration) lasts for *AverageIllnessDuration* = 15 days.

- Recovered people are immune to the disease.

# Phase 1. Creating a stock and flow diagram

1.  Create a new model by selecting **File | New | Model** from the menu, and then name the model **SEIR**.

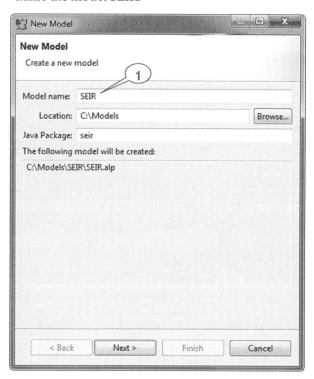

2.  Don't use the model template - click **Next** and then **Finish**.

Let's start with drawing stock and flow diagram. To model an epidemic's progress, we need to reduce our population diversity. In this example, we'll consider four important characteristics:

- *Susceptible* - people who are not infected by the virus

- *Exposed* - people who are infected but who can't infect others

- *Infectious* - people who are infected and who can infect others

- *Recovered* – people who have recovered from the virus

SEIR is an acronym that represents the four stages: Susceptible-Exposed-Infectious-Recovered.

There are four stocks in our model - one for each stage.

3. Drag four **Stocks** from the **System Dynamics** palette on to the diagram, and then name them *Susceptible, Exposed, Infectious*, and *Recovered*.

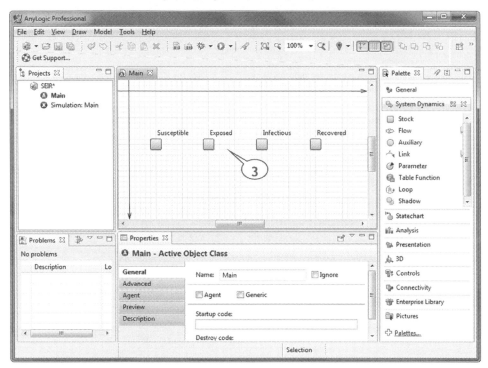

## Stocks and flows

In System Dynamics, *stocks* (also known as levels, accumulations, or state variables) represent real-world stocks of material, knowledge, people, money, etc. *Flows* define their rate of change - how stock values change and define the system's dynamics. Here are some examples of stocks and flows:

| Stock | Inflows | Outflows |
|---|---|---|
| **Population** | Births<br>Immigration | Deaths<br>Emigration |
| **Fuel tank** | Refueling | Fuel consumption |

Flow may flow out of one stock and flow in another. Such a flow is outflow for the first stock and inflow for the second one at the same time, see the figure below:

Flow may flow into a stock from nowhere. In this case the cloud (denoting "source") is drawn at the flow's starting point.

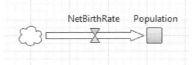

And symmetrically, flow may flow out from a stock to "nowhere". In this case the cloud (denoting "sink") is drawn at the flow's end point.

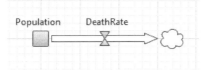

The flow's arrow shows its direction.

In our model, susceptible people are exposed to the virus, become infectious, and then recover. It's a progression that requires our model to use three flows to drive people from one stock to the next.

4.  Add the first flow that flows from the stock *Susceptible* to *Exposed*. Double-click the stock where the flow flows out (*Susceptible*), and then click the stock where it flows in (*Exposed*).

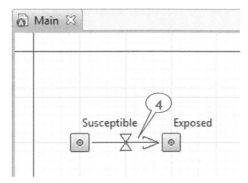

5.    Name the flow *ExposedRate.*

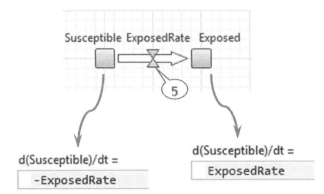

6.    You can look at the formulas of *Susceptible* and *Exposed* stocks. Since our *ExposedRate* flow reduces the value of *Susceptible* stock and increases *Exposed,* the formulas should be the same as in the figures below. AnyLogic automatically created these formulas when you added the flow.

## Formulas of stocks

AnyLogic automatically generates a stock's formula according to the user's stock-and-flow diagram.

Stock value is calculated according to flows flowing in and out from the stock. The value of inflows – the flows that increase stock value – are added and the value of outflows – flows that reduce the stock – are subtracted from the stock's current value:

*inflow1 + inflow2 ... - outflow1 - outflow2 ...*

In the classic system, dynamics notation only flows can appear in the formula. The formula is non-editable and no other elements other than flows flowing in and out the stock can appear in the formula.

7.    Add a flow from *Exposed* to *Infectious* , and then name it *InfectiousRate.*

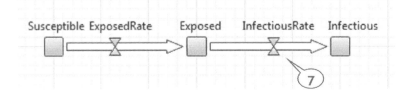

8. Add a flow from *Infectious* to *Recovered*, and then name it *RecoveryRate*.

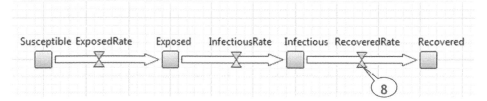

9. Rearrange the flow names as shown in the figure below. To do this, select a flow and then drag its name.

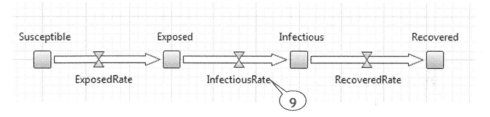

10. Now, let's define the parameters and dependencies. Add five **Parameters**, name them, and then define their default values according to the information below:

- *TotalPopulation* = 10 000

- *Infectifity* = 0.6

- *ContactRateInfectious* = 1.25

- *AverageIncubationTime* = 10

- *AverageIllnessDuration* = 15

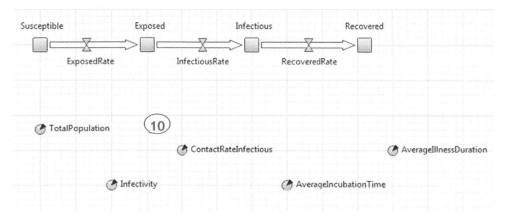

11. Define the number of infected people by specifying *1* as the **Initial Value** of the stock *Infectious.*

12. Define the **Initial Value** for the stock *Susceptible*: *TotalPopulation-1.*

You may press Ctrl+space (Mac OS: Alt+space) and then select the parameter's name from the Code Completion assistant.)

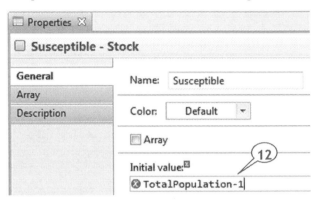

You'll see the red sign to the expression's left. The reason for the problem is you've defined a dependency between two elements in the stock and flow diagram (the stock *Susceptible*'s initial value depends on the parameter *TotalPopulation*), but this dependency is not defined graphically as it should be.

## Dependency links

Stock and flow diagrams have two types of dependencies:

- An element (stock, flow, auxiliary, or parameter) is mentioned in a flow or auxiliary's formula. This link type is drawn with a solid line:

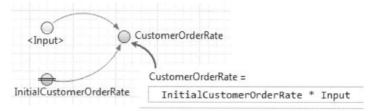

- An element is mentioned in the stock's initial value. This link type is drawn with a dotted line:

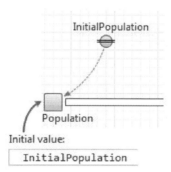

You should use *links* to graphically define dependencies among a stock and flow diagram's elements.

If an element *A* is mentioned in the equation or element *B*'s initial value, you should first connect these elements with a link from *A* to *B* and then type the expression in *B*'s properties.

**13.** Draw a dependency link from *TotalPopulation* to *Susceptible*:

In the **System Dynamics** palette, double-click the **Link** element, click *TotalPopulation*, and then click the stock *Susceptible*. You should see the link with small circles drawn on its end points:

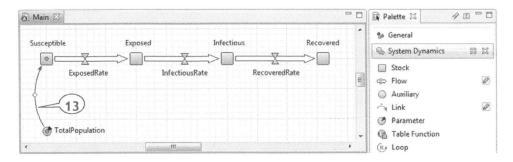

14. Let's define the formula for the flow *ExposedRate*.

    Click the flow and define the following formula using the Code Completion assistant:

    *Infectious\*ContactRateInfectious\*Infectivity\*Susceptible/TotalPopulation*

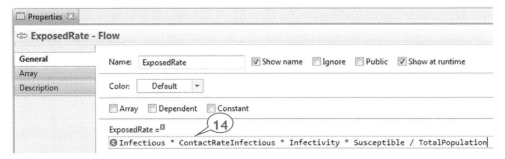

15. Click in the formula field, and you'll see the error indicator to formula's left.

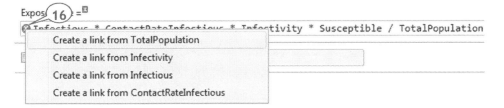

We need to draw dependency links from the mentioned variables and parameters to this flow. You may find it tedious to manually draw the links, so we'll show you how to add links using AnyLogic's link auto-creation mechanism.

16. Click the error indicator. AnyLogic's menu lists the problems and their likely solutions.

17. Select the list's items one by one to create all the missing links. Afterward, you should see the links in the stock and flow diagram:

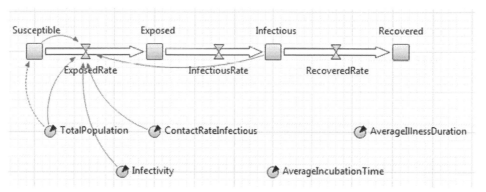

18. Define the following formula for *InfectiousRate*:
    *Exposed/AverageIncubationTime*

19. Define the following formula for *RecoveryRate*:
    *Infectious/AverageIllnessDuration*

20. Draw the missing dependency links, and your stock and flow diagram should resemble the following image:

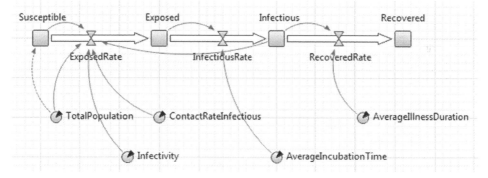

21. Adjust the appearance of dependency links. Modify the links' bend angles to make the diagram match the figure below. To adjust the link's bend angle, select it, and then drag the handle in the middle of the link.

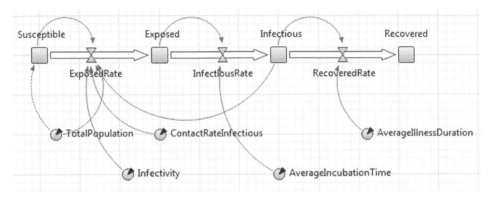

22. Run the model and inspect the dynamics using the variables' inspect windows. To open a variable's inspect window, click the variable to select it. To resize the window, drag its lower right corner.

23. To switch the inspect window to the plot mode, click the leftmost icon in its toolbar.

24. Increase the model execution speed to make the simulation go faster.

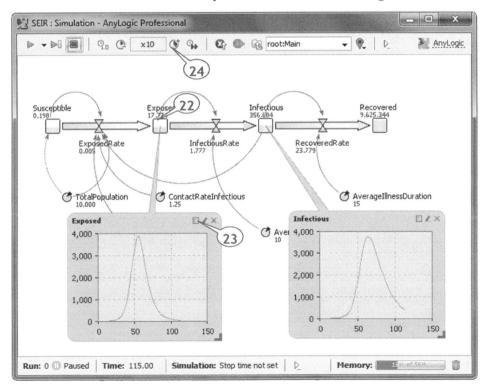

# Phase 2. Adding a plot to visualize dynamics

*Feedback loops: balancing and reinforcing*

System dynamics studies causal dependencies in systems. There are two types of feedback loops: *reinforcing* and *balancing*.

Here are some hints how to know the loop type (taken from Wikipedia).

To determine if a causal loop is reinforcing or balancing, start with an assumption such as "*VariableN* increases," and then follow the loop.

The loop is:

- *reinforcing* if, after going around the loop, you get the same result as the initial assumption.

- *balancing* if the result contradicts the initial assumption.

You can also use the alternate definition:

- *reinforcing* loops have an even number of negative links (zero also is even)

- *balancing* loops have an uneven number of negative links.

We'll add a loop identifier for one loop to show you.

1.  Drag the **Loop** element from the **System Dynamics** palette on to the diagram, and then place it as shown in the figure.

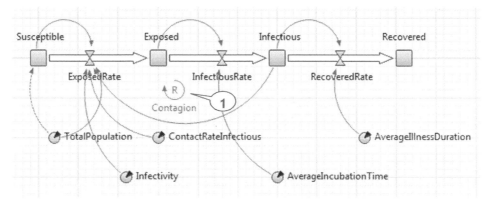

2.  Go to the loop's **Properties**, change its **Type** to **R** (stands for Reinforcing), leave the default **Clockwise Direction**, and specify the text AnyLogic will display near the loop icon: *Contagion*.

## Loop identifiers

*Loop* is a graphical identifier with a label that briefly describes the loop's meaning and an arrow that shows the loop's direction.

Rather than defining the causal loop, it provides information about how your stock and flow diagram's variables affect one another. By adding loops, you can help other users understand the stock and flow diagram's influences and causal dependencies.

*Contagion* loop is reinforcing. An increase in *Infectious* leads to an increase of *ExposedRate*, which in turn leads to a greater increase of *Exposed.* All links in this loop are positive.

Please find out what are other loops in this stock and flow diagram. What are their directions and types?

Let's add a time chart to plot Susceptible, Exposed, Infectious, and Recovered people.

3. Drag the **Time Plot** from the **Analysis** palette on to the diagram.

4. Extend the time plot as shown in the figure below.

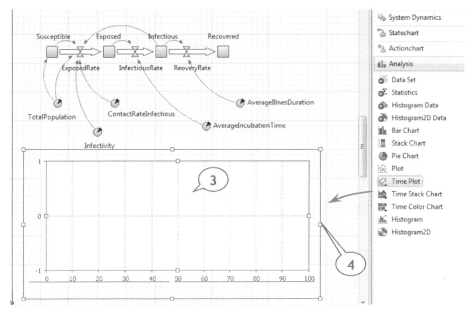

5. In the **Properties** view, click **Add data item**.

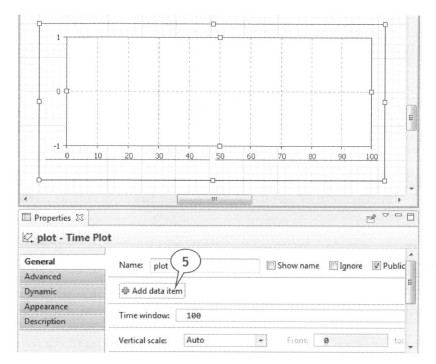

6. Modify the data item's properties:

- **Title:** *Susceptible people* – title of the data item.

- **Value:** *Susceptible* (use *Code Completion Master*).

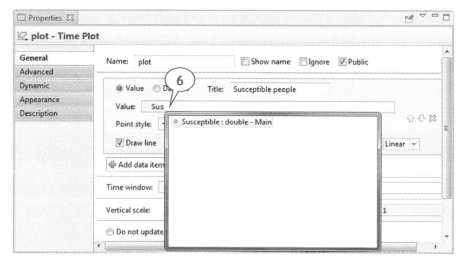

7.  Add three data items to display the values of stocks *Exposed*, *Infectious*, and *Recovered* in the same way - and don't forget to define the corresponding **Titles**.

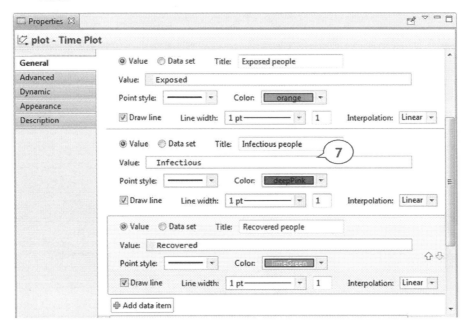

8.  We've finished our last model. Now, run the model and use the chart you added to view its dynamics.

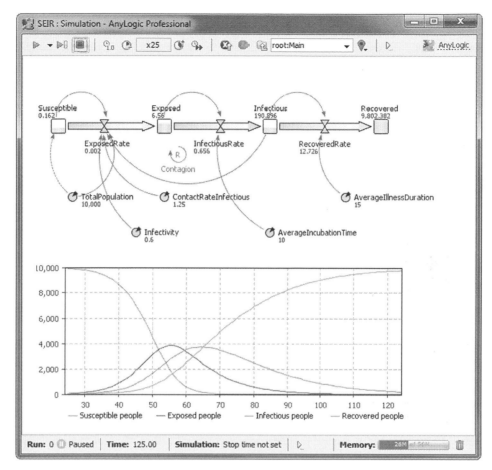

We think you're ready to continue creating models. To take that next step, use AnyLogic Help and AnyLogic How-To example models which allow you to find implementations of specific modeling techniques.

As you evaluate AnyLogic, you can use the **Get Support** button to ask our Support Team for technical assistance, for help using our program, or for help using your models. If you purchase AnyLogic, you'll receive a license that entitles you to a full year of technical support.

Made in the USA
Charleston, SC
30 December 2012